While Healing Comes

LoriAnn,

What a divine appointment! God is good and I'm so glad we crossed paths!

♡ Faye!

PRAISE FOR WHILE HEALING COMES

I couldn't put this book down! There was hard truth, but somehow at the same time, it was filled with a great hope. Faye's ability to be transparent and honest with herself and with God is proof of an amazing relationship with the Father. What a privilege to have the whole story giving us all courage to endure. I have the gift of knowing Stephanie and I am excited for others to know her as well! The world is a much better place because she is here. Thank you, Mom and Dad Doudak, for fighting the good fight on her behalf. My bravery as a parent has been multiplied because of you.

—LAURIE WESTWOOD
Bethel SOZO Regional Facilitator for DE, NJ, NY and PA
Bethel SOZO Team Leader at The House of Praise in Greenwood, DE

A heart-gripping book from the very first page, *While Healing Comes* depicts the heart of every mother who has struggled with the diagnosis of a special needs child. I was overwhelmed with emotions—I cried and mourned Deborah's death with Faye. I felt anger at a hospital's neglect that turned into a mom's worse nightmare and resulted in Stephanie's fight to survive. I wanted to run to this woman, hug her, cry with her, and thank her for putting on paper what parents in similar situations experience—for being the voice of hope. This is not a book of trauma and self-pity, but of hope and faith, it is a book of healing and surrender.

Faye's decision to trust the God who had spoken to her early in the journey and to put her faith into action was inspiring. *While Healing Comes* challenges us to trust the God who never leaves us nor forsakes us. She introduces us to a God who carries us when life gets hard, and empowers us to face the challenges and difficulties of parenting and life in general. This is a beautiful read!

—PASTOR MILLIE MERCADO
Shepherding Pastor & Director of Ministries, Resurrection Church in New York, NY

While Healing Comes shares true experiences coming from a heart like Abraham: a heart which took all types of risk for the sake of being obedient. It comes from a heart like Moses: a heart willing to face any challenge for the sake of choosing God's paths. Faye has made choices like Abraham and Moses in the toughest times of her life. Her story of struggle and victory will strengthen you and give you courage for whatever you must face.

I met Faye 18 years ago when Stephanie was just a few months old. I was touched by her hunger to be filled with the Holy Spirit and to walk by faith not by sight. I am constantly moved by her deep desire to welcome God's will in her life. Her sincere pursuit to know God's character—to know Him for who He is and to understand His ways—has encouraged me to join her in the journey of faith. We became best friends in very short time and I have watched her remain true to herself while facing pain, even while expressing her frustration when she feels that she has no control over things. I have watched her side-by-side, choosing in many situations to have David's attitude saying: *"Why, my soul, are you downcast? Why so disturbed within me? Put your hope in God, for I will yet praise him, my Savior and my God"* (Psalm 43:5, NIV).

I admire how Faye surrenders her ways and allows God's hand to use the pain to form who she has become today: a woman of faith, a voice of worship for God filled with songs of praise for His faithfulness. She grew a lot while being a warrior in the narrow path, and was strengthened by faith … all the while giving glory to God. I grew in my faith because I was part of Faye's journey. I have had the privilege of pushing her forward and challenging her to put her trust in God from one phase to another. Faye's persistence, strong will, and determination to work hard toward greatness has caused her to become a great coach to several woman struggling in different areas. That same tenacity and pursuit of joy will uplift and encourage you in your own journey.

—MERVAT GUBRAEL
Mentor & Best Friend

Faye is one of the most authentic, real, and powerful women I know. She has paid the price for what she has. I honor, respect, and aspire to live as she does in her love for God and others. In *While Healing Comes*, she simply and powerfully shares truth and revelation without holding anything back. She challenges anything that prevents a person from being fully free, loved, and living to their full potential.

Faye is a mama who will go to any length to see that her child will live out who they are and are treated as such. This book is an invitation not to settle for less than what God has for you and your family. It will take you into the deep truth and dynamics of what life with a special needs child is like; the reality of fear, doubt, and hopelessness it may bring. But she does not leave you there, she brings you to the other side of how to come to live with it peacefully. Not only that, but also how to bravely believe for and fight for healing.

Anyone who reads this book will walk away a better person, with greater revelation centered on the truth that regardless of your situation, you are free to choose to allow God to love you and guide you. He will keep His promise that He will never leave you nor forsake you. I believe *While Healing Comes* will help people access JESUS—in revelation, in truth, in love, in healing, and in freedom.

—AFNAN LIBERTY LIEB

Founder & Director of Beauty 4 Ashes Dance School
Director of Women's Ministry, East Gate Church
BA Family Studies, Interpreter for CCIU PA

Offering a rare glimpse into the true reality faced by a family coping with a special needs child, *While Healing Comes* is raw and authentic. Infused with the author's unwavering faith in God and the hope of His promise, I was most struck by the outpoured grace so apparent in the life of this brave woman. The depth of character evident in her because of this incredible journey is both admirable and inspiring. With so much that could make her a victim and paralyze her joy, Faye has instead become a shining light of God's expressed glory. This story will move you in unexpected ways.

—WENDY K. WALTERS
Author of Intentionality, Live on Purpose!
Motivational Speaker, Master Coach
Director, The Favor Foundation

$\mathcal{S}$TEPHANIE'S $\mathcal{S}$TORY

While Healing Comes

OUR BATTLE TO OVERCOME CEREBRAL PALSY

Faye Doudak
CNHP, ND

© 2018 Faye Doudak. All Rights Reserved.
While Healing Comes

All Rights Reserved. This book is protected by the copyright laws of the United States of America. This book may not be copied or reprinted for commercial gain or profit. The use of short quotations is permitted. Permission will be granted upon request. The author guarantees all contents are original and do not infringe upon the legal rights of any other person or work.

Printed in the USA

ISBN (print): 978-1-7323428-0-4

ISBN (kindle): 978-1-7323428-1-1

Prepared for Publication by www.palmtreeproductions.com

To contact the author: www.fayedoudak.com

On Facebook: Faye Doudak

DEDICATION

Stephanie—

I am grateful for your life and sacrifice. You are a shining star, a powerful woman of God. Thank you for being who you are despite the pain and frustration. I wish you were able to tell your story with your own words, but I believe the day will come when you will. Meanwhile, allow me to write a prelude.

Ted—

I am so thankful for my awesome husband, you have been a rock and a refuge for my weary soul throughout the years. After Christ, you are my everything. Thank you for loving us the way you do.

Rebecca, Theodore, and Daniel—

Thank you for being understanding and flexible. Thank you for putting up with the chaos, hospital visits, canceled vacations, and uncertainties. Thank you for being the best siblings: including learning how to care for your sister, even attending to her seizures and emergencies. Thank you for not complaining or rebelling. You are the AWESOMEST children a mother could have.

Kim—

Thank you for being a second mother. Thank you for the sleepless nights, all the shed tears, and bottomless love. Thank you for being there every time I needed you.

Mom—

You are the best. Thank you for the emotional and spiritual support. Thank you for all your prayers and encouragement. Thank you for all the delicious meals.

Dad, my brothers, Ted's family—

I can't say thank you enough to each of you. I appreciate your support and kind gestures.

Extended family and friends—

This space is not large enough to list all your names, but I will never forget your stand with us. Thank you for your prayers and good thoughts. Thank you for encouraging me to write this book. I would not be who I am today without the community of people that surrounds me.

From the depths of my soul, thank you. I am eternally grateful.

SPECIAL THANKS

Throughout the years we were blessed by people who came alongside us and supported us in our time of need. We are grateful for such people and I want to express my gratitude by mentioning their names here.

- Thank you to all the kind nurses and doctors at the NICU and PICU. Thank you for being patient and doing your best to attend to my daughter.

- Dr. Preis, you are one of a kind. You always take your time to joke around with her. You never treated her as a disabled child. You know she loves you.

- John and the staff of Farmacon Pharmacy: You guys are awesome. Thank you for being there for us every time we needed a prescription filled. You always made sure we never ran out of medications.

- Regina and the staff of RFC: I can't say thank you enough for all your help throughout the years. Thank you for sticking with us through all the insurance ups and downs. You made our life much easier.

- Ellen Doman and the National Association of Child Development: Thank you for giving us the hope to fight for Stephanie. Thank you for encouraging us to pursue a better future for her.

- Matthew and Carol Newell and the staff of the Family Hope Center: Thank you for opening up new possibilities for us. Thank you for pushing us out of our comfort zone.

- Nick Riccio: You were a gift sent from heaven. Thank you for always grounding me in my time of trouble. You always knew the right answer to my dilemmas. I will greatly miss you my friend.

- Debra Nicolosi at Natural Allergy Solutions: If it wasn't for you, Stephanie would still be struggling with mucus over production. You saved us a lot of trouble and hospital visits.

- Our family members and friends: There are no words that can express our gratitude for your love, support and encouragement. You were a lifesaver when the waters became too rough.

- Mervat G.: God sent you to mentor me at the right time. You walked with me for years. Thank you for being strong enough to keep me on the straight and narrow. Thank you for knowing when to encourage me and when to kick my behind.

- Dr. Tabick: If it wasn't for you, Stephanie wouldn't be able to hold her head up. Thank you for being brave to work on her. You changed her life and the way she sees the world.

Finally, I want to thank all the people who prayed for us through all the trials. Thank you for the encouraging words that strengthened my faith. I appreciate your support.

CONTENTS

ix	DEDICATION	
xi	SPECIAL THANKS	
xiii	CONTENTS	
1	CHAPTER ONE	*Pregnancy and Birth*
7	CHAPTER TWO	*Meeting Deborah*
11	CHAPTER THREE	*First Three Months*
17	CHAPTER FOUR	*Brain Damage*
23	CHAPTER FIVE	*After the Brain Damage*
29	CHAPTER SIX	*Sleeping Beauty*
41	CHAPTER SEVEN	*Why?*
51	CHAPTER EIGHT	*Heart to Heart*

| 61 | CHAPTER NINE
Therapies |
| 71 | CHAPTER TEN
Family Dynamics |
| 77 | CHAPTER ELEVEN
Daniel's Story |
| 87 | CHAPTER TWELVE
Still Waiting |
| 95 | PHOTO GALLERY
Stephanie in Pictures |
| 115 | MEET THE AUTHOR
Faye Doudak |

CHAPTER ONE
Pregnancy and Birth

In the early part of 1999, I found out that I was pregnant for the third time. I already had an amazing five-year old girl and a brilliant two-year old son. My husband loved children and he wanted as many of them as possible. I, on the other hand, was not so crazy about having so many children. I did not mind the raising up part, but the pregnancy and delivery were a different story. As soon as I found out I was pregnant, I started praying for twins. I figured two babies for the price of one was a smart idea. You can't imagine my joy and relief when, a few weeks later, the doctor told me I was carrying twins indeed. It was an amazing surprise to the whole family. Everyone started anticipating the arrival of the twins immediately, especially the children.

In July of the same year, the children and I went on a trip overseas to visit my family. We spent three wonderful weeks over there. I was doing fine. The pregnancy was normal and everything moved along as scheduled. Upon returning to New York, however, I started noticing unusual symptoms. I called the doctor and made an appointment to see him Friday the same week. Early Friday, before my appointment, I started having contractions. I was a couple of days over twenty-three weeks gestation. Worried, I hurried to the doctor's office to see what was going on. The doctor was alarmed and rushed me off to the hospital.

On Friday, August 27, I was admitted to the Methodist Hospital in an attempt to stop the premature labor. Doctors administered IV drugs trying to stop the contractions. However, despite their efforts, Deborah was born later that night at twenty-three and a half weeks gestation. She weighed less than 550 grams, less than 20 ounces. She was transferred to NY Presbyterian Hospital in Manhattan.

My husband was with me throughout everything. Ted stayed by my side, held my hand, and wiped my tears. He prayed with and for me. He patiently observed as Deborah was born and was the first to see her when she was placed in the incubator. He was reassuring and peaceful while I tried to make sense of what was going on. His strength and stability sustained me through the first delivery.

Fortunately, the twins were in different sacs and the doctors were able to keep Stephanie in utero. They continued to administer IV drugs to relax my womb. The doctors also gave me a shot or two of corticosteroids to help the remaining baby develop stronger lungs. They were hoping with bed rest and medications, the baby would remain in utero for at least another 3-6 weeks.

That did not happen. The drugs had a side effect on my body. They sped up my heart rate to the point where I felt my heart beating in my fingertips. I could not speak or move. The blood was pumping so fast I started hemorrhaging on Monday.

Ted came to see me Monday afternoon. He had just left me to go to NY Presbyterian Hospital when the hemorrhaging started. I bled so fast my water broke within minutes. The nurses rushed in, and immediately called both my doctor and my husband. They were prepping me for delivery and waiting on my doctor to arrive when Ted showed up. We did not think we would have another traumatic experience so soon after Deborah's birth.

As a result of too much blood loss, I lost my ability to communicate in English. I could only speak in Arabic and Ted had to translate for me. My body was under so much stress my brain just retreated to its default settings.

It seemed like eternity before my doctor showed up, because he had been delivering another baby. Meanwhile, I found myself surrounded by more than a dozen doctors who came to observe this rare case. It was embarrassing and uncomfortable having all those people taking advantage of a living learning moment. I kept asking to be covered. I felt exposed like a lab rat.

Finally, my OB/GYN arrived but was hesitant to rush me in for an emergency C-Section because my platelet count was too low. He was afraid I would lose too much blood. I was already going in and out of consciousness due to the blood loss. They could not get an accurate ultrasound of the baby because the embryonic fluids were almost drained. The doctor did a manual check and found the baby laying horizontally. He tried to rotate her but the placenta was positioned in his way. Fearing he would rupture it, he realized I had no hope for another natural delivery. He ordered the operating room to be made ready for me. At the same time, a hematologist was checking my clotting time. She was cutting my arm in different places and then applying a special paper over the cut to determine the clotting time. Again, they were worried I would bleed too much during surgery. Nonetheless, I was wheeled into the O.R. on Monday evening for an emergency C-section.

Stephanie was born on Aug 30, 1999 weighing about 645 grams (almost 23 ounces). Like her sister, she was also transferred to the NICU of NY Presbyterian Hospital, although each girl was placed in a different room. Back at Methodist Hospital I was given two units of blood during surgery and immediately afterwards I developed a fever. The doctors were confused and called in a specialist from the infectious diseases department. He concluded the blood I was given earlier was infected with some strain of bacteria. I was placed on strong IV antibiotic for a few days. The antibiotic levels were required to be monitored on a daily basis. The nurse drew blood before and after each dosage. The medicine was so strong it felt like Clorox running through my veins. By the time I left the hospital, my arms had large patches of black and blue skin. My body hurt so much from delivering twice in three days, bleeding, the C-section, and fighting off the infection. But my heart was hurting even more. I constantly thought about the two tiny girls fighting for their lives in the incubators across town. Ted was going back and forth checking on me and them. He updated me on their status. I remember him trying to stress the fact that I should not be surprised when I got to finally see them.

"They don't look like newborn babies. They are too small," he would say repeatedly.

> NOTHING HE SAID PREPARED ME FOR HOW I FELT WHEN I VISITED THEM FOR THE FIRST TIME

He did not want me to be shocked by how tiny they were. Nothing he said prepared me for how I felt when I visited them for the first time.

On Friday, September 4, I was released from the hospital. The fever had gone away and it seemed I was doing fine. Within four days I had more complications directly related to the infection. I was constrained to my room on the second floor since I was not allowed to go up and down the stairs. Tuesday morning, I made my way to the bathroom and noticed drops of blood on the floor. Immediately, I unwrapped my robe to check on the incision. Sure enough, the incision had gotten infected too. Pus gathered on the inside and pushed against the stitches to the point of breaking them open. My mom was in the kitchen downstairs and came scurrying as soon as she heard my scream. Thankfully, at the same moment, my brother was walking in the door to check on me. He carried me from the bathroom and laid me back in my bed. I had to be rushed back to the hospital by an ambulance. In cases like this, the doctors leave the wound open to give it a chance to heal on its own from the inside out. All they do is stuff it with gauze. Because of my low platelet count, my wounds took a longer time than usual to adhere. For about a month, I had an open incision in my tummy stuffed with gauze.

This was not my worst situation by far. Deborah died just two weeks after her birth. Doctors said she was so small and underdeveloped, and even though she was in an incubator, she did not have accessible veins to deliver all the meds and nutrients required to sustain her. The only access point was her umbilical cord which was not enough to transport all that was needed to keep her alive.

A Fighting Chance

I only got to see her once! Thank God, Stephanie got a fighting chance. She was a bit larger and the steroids helped her lungs. The doctors were able to establish an A-line in her inner thigh and a Broviac (Hickman) Catheter directly to her heart. In addition, she had one or two IV lines in her body. This enabled them to reach her with all the meds and fluids she needed to survive. When she was ready, they added a nasogastric tube to deliver the formula into her stomach. Stephanie was in the NICU for about three months. She was released on December 3, 1999 weighing almost four and a half pounds.

The first three months after the delivery were charged with opposing emotions. It all depended on the hospital's report of the girls' health. I went through cycles of anger, fear, hope, peace, doubt and relief on a daily basis. The first and last thing I did every day was to call the hospital to check on them. For the first two weeks, I was not physically able to leave the house to visit them. I relied solely on the phone calls and my husband's report. In addition to the emotional rollercoaster, I was having nightmares every time I went to sleep. The same dream repeated itself every night. I was traveling on a train with my twins in my arms. Then all of a sudden, I would take out a knife and start cutting them in pieces and throwing them overboard. I would wake up terrified, screaming and sweating. The torture was unbearable. My doctor suggested sleeping pills, but I was afraid I would become dependent on them.

The only thing that brought me some relief was falling asleep listening to worship music. I don't remember when the nightmares stopped exactly, but it was months before I could sleep for three or four hours straight without violently waking up.

CHAPTER TWO
Meeting Deborah

The girls were almost two weeks old when I saw them for the first time since their premature births. Ted rolled me in the wheelchair up to the sixth floor at NY Presbyterian Hospital where the Neonatal Intensive Care Unit was located. They were held in two separate rooms and I went to see Deborah first. I can't describe my feelings when I laid eyes on her. She was naked in the incubator, her eyes shut, and wires stuck out of her body in every direction. They monitored her heartbeat, blood pressure and breathing. A tube was secured to her mouth by white tape. It extended from her trachea to the humming ventilation machine that stood nearby. She could not breathe on her own yet; she needed assistance. The lights were dim which made the monitors seem even brighter. Doctors, nurses and therapists moved around in sync doing their part and communicating softly with each other. The room felt cold and the beeping sounds played their own song.

Ted left me for a few moments to speak to the doctors. I couldn't control my tears as I came closer to the incubator. She didn't look like a newborn baby. Her fingers stood up like little stubs from the palm of her hands and her toes were like little dots at the end of her feet. Her face was pale and scrawny. Millions of thoughts were racing in my mind and I was overtaken by emotions and tears. I started to wheel myself out the door when an older nurse grabbed me.

"Where are you going?" she asked.

"I am leaving. I am not ready for this." I answered.

She stood in front of me and motioned me back toward the incubator. My face was covered with tears by this point. We exchanged stares silently but she did not back down. I turned myself around and headed towards Deborah.

As she walked alongside me, she whispered, "You have to touch and talk to her."

I parked in front of the incubator and stared at the still baby. I don't think she even acknowledged my presence. The nurse reached out for my arm and wedged my hand through the round opening. Silent tears turned into loud sobbing as I stroked her body with my fingers. Her skin felt cold and tense and there was no response to my touch.

I calmed myself a bit so I could talk to her. The nurse said I would regret it if she died before I told her how I felt.

"Mommy loves you so much. Please forgive me for not carrying you to full term. I wish I could take your pain." I stopped for a moment, then continued, "I want you to fight and get stronger, but I won't blame you if you choose to be with Jesus instead."

I wanted her to stay but I also didn't want to her to suffer or feel bad about leaving me. I stayed by her incubator for a while trying to sort out my emotions. Pain, sorrow and guilt squeezed my heart and laid heavy on my chest. I prayed for her silently. Then in the midst of the explosive emotions, I felt the peace of God washing over my body. I let out a sigh of relief and released Deborah into His arms. Before I left the room, the attending doctor made sure I understood her chances of surviving were very slim.

The next day, I sat in my armchair and thought about the girls as I dialed the hospital's number. This had been my routine for the previous two weeks. I called every two hours, day and night, to get the latest report on their progress. The nurse on the other end on the line assured me all was well. There were no changes since the last time I had called. I was confined to my chair because of the open incision in my abdomen. There wasn't much to do to keep my mind busy. I couldn't escape the war on my thoughts and emotions as I waited to hear the next report. About an hour later, the phone rang.

"This is NY Presbyterian Hospital. May I speak to Mr. or Mrs. Doudak?" The lady asked.

My heart sank and my mouth went dry as I handed the phone to Ted. I knew from the look on his face that something was wrong.

"I'll be right there, ma'am," Ted said as he hung up the phone.

I begged him not to say anything. I was already crying.

He knelt on the floor, held my hands and with tears streaming on his cheeks he said, "Deborah is gone."

I sat on my bedroom floor and cried quietly for a long time. No words can express how I felt then. It felt like a piece of me was ripped off. My whole being was bleeding. Every cell in my body was screaming in pain. A volcano of anger exploded in my core and I screamed at God. I blamed Him for everything. I told Him I was done with Him, that I didn't want Him anymore. This was unfair! I don't deserve this. What did I do wrong? Nothing else mattered at that moment. Life lost its meaning. The pain was too much and I wanted to die.

In the midst of my chaos I heard the still voice in my heart whispering, "I feel your pain, baby. It's always your choice to be with me or not. Whatever you decide I will always love you." He paused for a moment. "If you choose to trust me I will walk you through the dark times. You have a rough road ahead of you but I will walk with you if you allow me."

I came back to my senses and thought for a few seconds. There was no way I could go through this without Him. I was ready to give up. How could I wade through these murky waters alone? I needed Him to guide me in the valley stretching ahead of me.

"Please, help me, Father," I cried. Before I had even finished my sentence, I felt His embrace and a new season began.

Funeral arrangements were made quickly. Ted and a close friend accompanied our pastor to the cemetery where they laid her body in the ground. I couldn't go. Emotionally, I wasn't ready to accept the fact that she was gone so soon. I never even got to hold her or feel her breath on my skin. No kisses were blown, not enough "I love you's" were said. My arms ached for years longing to carry her. It took me ten years to visit her grave for the first time. Meanwhile, I was occupied with Stephanie's medical traumas and emergencies.

CHAPTER THREE

First Three Months

After Deborah's death, I put all my energy into being there for Stephanie. My husband and I took shifts visiting her in the NICU. The doctors hoped she had a better chance to make it than her sister. Apparently, she was the stronger one, weighing 100 grams more than Deborah. She had stayed in utero three extra days and the steroid shots had given her lungs a boost. She even looked a little healthier than her sister. However, she was still very small. Her head was the size of a lemon and her thigh was only as thick as her father's thumb, but Stephanie fought for her life from day one. She is the strongest person I know. Every day while she was in the NICU, I dropped the older children at school and drove to the city to be with her. I spent countless hours staring at the monitors while she laid helpless in the incubator. My heart sank every time I heard the loud beep indicating a drop in her heart rate or oxygen level.

Anxiety and fear were always close by ready to claw at my emotions. The hardest battle in those early days was to hold on to my faith and peace. I read to Stephanie, and sang to her. First, she was in an enclosed incubator. I was only allowed to put my hands in through the holes to touch her. Later, she laid in a special bed with overhead lights to keep her body warm since she couldn't regulate her body temperature on her own. At that stage, they allowed me to hold her on my bare skin to help her connect with me and form a bond. This practice also helped regulate her breathing by syncing it with my own breaths. I lived for those moments.

There were four or five premature babies in the room at a time. The other moms were going through the same experiences I was. Even though we tried to give each other some privacy, we longed to connect for emotional support. The truth was very few people outside the NICU understood what we were going through at that time. We found a haven in each other during our time in the hospital. We celebrated our babies' little milestones and were disappointed over their setbacks. The atmosphere was always emotionally charged. Life and death were in a constant battle in that room. Hope and despair walked hand in hand as one mom would be excited about taking her child home, while another would be crying over the loss of hers. Add to that my own emotional rollercoaster over Stephanie's progress, and you can imagine how exhausted I felt by the time I went home to mother my two children.

Sustaining a premature baby's life is a delicate matter. The doctors needed to create an environment as close to the womb as possible. Between delivering nutrition, sustaining the body's temperature, monitoring the breathing and a million other things, the variables changed from one hour to another. There was always the risk of infection. Gowns, gloves and face masks were required when we dealt with her. I learned how to read the monitors and the medical charts. I became exposed to new scientific vocabulary and concepts. I started to worry about oxygen and carbon dioxide levels. De-stating was a dreaded word in the NICU. It meant the baby was not breathing efficiently and the oxygen levels were coming down. Sometimes this meant the doctors would need to intubate her and hook her up to the ventilation machine. This was a major setback. Often, she would be so exhausted from breathing on her own, she would relax too much while on the ventilation and it would take a few days to get her off.

At first, she was totally dependent on the machine to breathe for her. Nutrients, fluids and meds were pumped into her body 24 hours a day via IV lines. One of the main concerns was to keep at least two IV lines open at the same time. Stephanie had small spidery veins. It was difficult for the technicians to start an IV line on her. They had to be very creative and patient. I was so disturbed by the IV lines sticking out of her neck or skull. Drawing blood was another obstacle. In the NICU it was a small prick in the heel. But later, it was torture to get a vein to respond. I would hold her down and attempt to comfort her for as long as an hour while nurses and doctors took turns to see who would be lucky to get an IV line going for Stephanie. When they finally found one, I would pray the line would not collapse before we left the hospital. At some point in the NICU they had an arterial line in her thigh and a Broviac catheter in the large vein leading directly into her heart. Stephanie also needed multiple blood transfusions while she was in the NICU. Her body was incapable of producing healthy blood cells at the rate needed for her to grow. She was constantly anemic. Ted and I were not a match. My uncle tried to donate blood but was declined too. We relied on the blood bank, and with my previous experience with a blood transfusion, you can imagine my feelings every time she needed one.

When they felt she was ready, they placed a nasogastric feeding tube to start giving her formula. This is a tube extending from a feeding pump, through her nose, down her esophagus and into her stomach. This was a huge step for her and we were thrilled. We were told she had to master a few things for her to be released. One of these was taking food by mouth and keeping the food down without vomiting. They started her with one cubic centimeter of formula stretched over an

> I CHOSE TO TRUST THAT HE WOULD KEEP HER ALIVE AND HEALTHY

hour and slowly increased it. One teaspoon is 5cc and a fluid ounce is 30cc. We anticipated the increase in her feeding capacity one cc at a time and her weight gain one gram at a time. The ups and downs of her progress took a toll on us. The doctors weren't sure she would make it even after all the efforts. Each day's outcome was uncertain. One time they were sure she might be blind or deaf. Another time they said she wouldn't live past six months. Every time I got a negative report from the doctors, I went home and talked to God about it. I chose to trust that He would keep her alive and healthy.

Her siblings were not allowed in the NICU for fear of introducing sickness and infection to the fragile preemies. Sometimes we brought them to the hospital to help them understand what was going on. They stayed in the family room with other children who were waiting on their parents. The first three months of Stephanie's life were rocky to say the least. We could not wait for her homecoming. Family members and friends supported us with prayer, babysitting the children, and preparing meals. We wouldn't have survived without all the support and love they provided. I can't talk about her time in the NICU without talking about the amazing staff at NY Presbyterian Hospital, especially the nurses. During our time there, we dealt with many doctors, specialists, and, of course, respiratory therapists. For the most part, they made themselves available to answer our questions and spared no effort to make sure Stephanie made it out of the NICU in the best shape possible. The nurses had the hardest job. They went above and beyond their job descriptions to make me feel at peace. They moved around the NICU like honeybees attending to each baby's needs. I am eternally grateful for the wonderful nurses that watched over my baby with care and kindness.

Three months felt like a lifetime while we waited for her to reach all the milestones required. There was a small period of training for me too. I was taught how to administer her medication, check her oxygen levels and perform CPR. She went through many tests to ensure her system was functioning properly. It included blood tests, as well as thorough CT scans and MRI screenings of her brain and internal organs. She passed all her tests. About two days before she was released, she was given a mixture of vaccinations including the Meningococcal vaccine. We were told she was doing well medically. Developmentally, she would be a year or two behind her peers, the doctors said. We didn't worry much about that. After all, in the grand scheme of life, what does it matter if she walks at age one or three? Finally, she was discharged to our care on December 3, 1999, weighing about four and a half pounds. We were ready to close the chapter and thought the worst was behind us.

WE THOUGHT THE
WORST WAS FINALLY
BEHIND US

CHAPTER FOUR
Brain Damage

At home for the first two weeks, I locked little Stephanie up in my bedroom. I wore my gown, gloves and face mask every time I entered the room. No one was allowed to come near her but my husband and me. The children observed from the hallway. I was totally terrified she would get sick. No visitors except my parents and brothers were allowed in the house.

Despite all the precautions, the first scare happened about two weeks after her discharge. Ted was at work, my mom was cooking dinner in the kitchen, the children were watching TV in the basement, and I needed to take a shower. I felt brave enough to venture with her outside my bedroom. I placed her on the sofa in the living room to take a nap while I ran upstairs to jump in the shower. Before I went up I alerted my mom to check on her in a few minutes. As I approached the middle of the staircase, I felt my heart squeeze and I knew I needed to go down to see if she was alright. She was not. She had stopped breathing and I could not detect her pulse. I never thought I would use my CPR training but it came in handy that day. It was a chaotic moment but surprisingly I stayed calm as I performed CPR on her and directed my non-English-speaking mom as she called 911. I could hear the sirens immediately.

Thankfully, the CPR worked and she regained consciousness moments before the paramedics arrived. All the way up until the police, fire department, and ambulance team arrived, I was well composed and unruffled. I was calm and level-headed while Stephanie's life was in my charge. However, the moment the EMT placed the oxygen on her face and assured me she would be fine, the whole thing hit me like a tsunami and I started to yell and jump up and down like a yo-yo. The fact was, I had just seen my daughter almost die and come back to life. The police officer tried to calm me down by saying I needed to put my shoes on so we could leave for the hospital. He finally held me by the shoulders, pressing them firmly for a few moments, before I came to my senses. I was totally numb but I put my shoes and jacket on and followed them to the ambulance. The drive to the hospital was short, 15 or 20 minutes at the most. I hovered over her the whole time, watching her breathing and listening to her heartbeat.

Once we arrived at the Maimonides Medical Center, the emergency room staff met us at the bay and escorted her inside. They took her medical history and then left us in the room for over 30 minutes without securing her to any monitors. I started feeling her breathing become more labored. Fearing she would stop breathing again, I yelled to get their attention to come and fasten a breathing monitor on her. They complied. At this point I was not confident they were competent enough to deal with a baby like mine. I asked to be transferred to NY Presbyterian Hospital. The nurse came back later saying that NY Presbyterian did not want to receive her (a lie, I found out later). After a few hours, they announced that she had an upper respiratory virus called Respiratory Syncytial Virus or RSV. She was admitted to the Pediatric Intensive Care Unit for a couple of days for observation. They provided her with oxygen via a nasal cannula during her stay. When they felt the danger had passed, they sent us home.

A Mother Knows...

A few days before Christmas, Stephanie started to act weird again. She was very lethargic and at one point had a fever of 104. I rushed her back to Maimonides Medical Center. They checked her and sent me home saying she was fine. The next day she got worse. She could hardly wake up and had no energy to suck on her bottle. In addition, a blue-grayish shadow started to form around her mouth. I sensed she was not getting enough oxygen and that scared me. I made the trip back to the ER. This time I brought my husband with me.

The ER staff was not happy to see me. In fact, they started to show me the door saying that I had no reason to worry. I proposed they do a standard blood and urine test on her. I even offered to pay for it in cash right then and there. After all, she was a 6-pound baby with a very complicated medical history of which they were aware. The intern checked with the attending doctor who said there was no need for the tests. They gently asked me to leave.

No one even looked at the half dead child in my arms. I was scared and in my heart, I knew that she would not last the night if she didn't get the proper care.

Being the stubborn woman that I am, I laid her in the crib, lifted the bars up, grabbed my husband and started walking out the door. I told them I did not feel comfortable taking care of her at home. They were shocked with my behavior but asked me to come back and promised to do the tests. Test results came back stating that she was extremely anemic and needed a blood transfusion. This did not put my heart at ease, but at least she was staying in the hospital now.

Again, we found ourselves in the PICU awaiting the blood from the bank. This would be transfusion number 15. Meanwhile, my gut was screaming that there was something else going on. I begged them to do a spinal tap.

"Anemia does not explain all her symptoms," I pleaded with the staff.

After verifying that I was not a medical doctor, they brushed my comments to the side.

Undeniable Symptoms

That evening I went home to check on my other children and as soon as I got home, the PICU nurse called to ask for my consent to do a spinal tap.

"What changed?" I asked.

"She is having seizures."

The seizures started right after I left her. Now they suspected there was something much worse than anemia going on. Naturally, I gave my consent. A few hours later the test confirmed that she had a group B bacterial meningitis in her brain and spinal fluids. They immediately started her on IV antibiotics, but it was too late. Forty-eight hours too late. The damage was already done. If only they had listened to me the day before …

I had never seen seizures before that day. They are scary and can unnerve you. They are not something you get used to no matter how many times you watch them happen. Stephanie still gets them to this day and even though we act calmly when they occur, we need time to recover emotionally from them afterwards. I don't know if it's the involuntary muscular twitching, the strange sounds she utters during an episode or the unseen damage you worry about them creating that causes you to unfold from the inside. Whatever the reason, seizures are not a welcomed episode in our home.

That night in the PICU, I stood helpless, watching her twitch and convulse non-stop. They started her on Phenobarbital immediately in an attempt to control the seizures. I could not even touch her because any slight interference would cause her to start seizing all over again. I remember waiting for hours before I could change her diaper for fear of seizures. At one point, I asked the nurse to come help me change it, and she yelled at me for being a lazy mother. It took the antibiotics about two days to deliver some relief. When she started to come about, she was no longer the same girl I had brought into the hospital four days prior.

"Unfortunately, there was some damage in the brain," one doctor told me on the fourth day. "Only time will tell what this means for your daughter." He apologized and left the room before his words sank into my mind.

This was not happening! I did not sign up for a brain-damaged child. *How am I going to deal with this?* I wondered, *What is this anyway?* Unanswered questions swarmed in my head that made me feel sick to my stomach. After attending to her needs and laying her down for a nap, I grabbed my Bible hoping to draw some peace from its pages. I poured my heart out to God and asked for His help facing this mountain.

I was led to read Daniel 2:21. *"He changes times and seasons; He deposes kings and raises up others. He gives wisdom to the wise and knowledge to the discerning."* He was promising me knowledge and wisdom to deal with the unknown. He was assuring me that this would be for a season and not permanent. A sense of peace engulfed me as I surrendered my mind to Him and thanked Him for being there for me.

Left to Ponder our Fate

The next day a neurologist came to see me in the PICU. She went over the events of the past five days making sure I understood what had happened. With obvious concern in her voice, she continued to explain to me the severity of the damage plaguing Stephanie's brain. I was told the meningitis had damaged the basal ganglia part of her brain. That part of the brain is responsible for voluntary motor control, procedural learning, and eye movement, as well as cognitive and emotional functions. Her words were abstract. I still did not understand what this meant for us.

Apparently, she sensed my confusion and started to speak to me in plain English.

"Your daughter's brain has no more control over her muscles. She will never be able to feed herself, hold a pen, or walk. Most likely, she won't be able to speak and will have a host of other problems. Only time will tell."

She then introduced me to the term "severe cerebral palsy" and left me to ponder the fate of my child in light of this new information.

We stayed in the hospital for a few more days until Stephanie was almost done with her antibiotics. We were sent home with care instructions and were set up with a couple of appointments for follow up with neurologists. She continued to take Phenobarbital to control the seizures.

Towards the end of 1999, the world was dealing with the Y2K scare. Meanwhile, I had to face my own fears of what the future was hiding for me and my family. The year started with the hope of life and an additional two members to our family. This was not the year's end that I had had in mind. However, I chose to trust in Father God and hope for a better tomorrow.

CHAPTER FIVE
After the Brain Damage

By the beginning of January 2000, Stephanie appeared the same to me. I didn't know what to expect or look for. What does brain damage look like after all? For a moment, I believed the doctors were mistaken. I hoped fervently they had misdiagnosed her and the whole thing was just a bad dream. But before I could take a breath from the drama of the previous four months, I started noticing small things that didn't make sense. Little by little she was losing her ability to suck on the bottle. Her lips started to weaken their grip on the nipple. Feeding time became a difficult task. Half of her food would run down her cheeks into the bib. I had to estimate how much she had eaten to determine if she needed to eat more. It took her 2-3 hours to finish a 3-ounce bottle of formula.

Soon after that she also developed severe acid reflux. It was so bad that two or three times a day, as soon as she had finished eating, the food would shoot out of her mouth like a missile. Frustrated, I would wash her up, change my clothes, clean the mess and start the 3-hour feeding session again, hoping that the food would stay down this time.

I wish I could say this was the worst of it. By the third week of January, a new symptom developed. It started slowly as a soft, constant whimper. Then it became a louder, whining cry. In about ten days, it developed into a consistent shrieking scream. The last stage was a loud scream with a forceful back bend of her head and spine. These episodes lasted a minimum of six hours. When she got too exhausted to scream, she would drop down and take a nap for an hour before starting all over again. Nothing we did soothed her. We tried all the tricks in the books. From rocking to singing to leaving her alone to taking her for walks in the stroller, nothing seemed to work.

I visited her pediatrician a few times in hope of finding out what was wrong. He had no clue what was going on. For several hours a day I carried her on my arm with one hand holding on to her head. I tried to protect her neck by resisting against her back with my hand to the point the nerves in my wrist became inflamed and painful. Carrying her around continually became my daily routine. I did all my house cleaning and cooking holding her while she screamed non-stop. Ted would take over for a few hours in the evening while I attended to the other children. We even hosted prayer meetings and gatherings in the house with her in our arms screaming. During the week, I took the night shift so Ted could sleep a little before work the next morning. I remember spending my nights carrying her in my arms and pacing in the living room waiting for her to get exhausted and sleep so I could rest briefly. During that time, I averaged seven to ten hours of sleep per week.

This lasted for about seven weeks, during which time I started to notice that her forehead was growing too large. The doctor seemed unconcerned and thought I was imagining things. He attributed her screaming to her neurological state. One night the screaming was so bad that I broke down and started crying myself. I sat on the living room floor with her in my lap. I couldn't take the painful look on her face anymore. Her eyes were looking at me as if begging me to help her and to ease the pain. Feeling powerless and in desperate need for some sleep, I cried out to God.

"Please, I beg you to take me home right now. If you really love me, don't let me see the light of day again. I can't do this anymore."

I just sat there and repeated that again and again. We both cried ourselves to sleep that night. When I woke up a few minutes later, I figured God hadn't answered my prayer. Scared of my mental state and what I had wished for, I was determined to figure out what was wrong with her.

> I WAS DETERMINED TO FIGURE OUT WHAT WAS WRONG WITH HER

Once again, I found myself at the doctor's office seeking answers. This time I was not going to leave until he could offer a solution. Fortunately, at this point he agreed with me that her forehead seemed larger than usual. Immediately, he called Maimonides Medical Center and informed them that Stephanie was coming in for an emergency MRI scan of the head. I felt uneasy as I walked back into that emergency room. It had been only 3 months since they had misdiagnosed her. I hadn't had time to process and go through forgiveness yet. I stuffed my emotions down as I'd been doing since August, and I promised myself I would deal with them as soon as I got the chance to do so. Soon the MRI results came in and they knew right away what was wrong.

A New Diagnosis

She was suffering from hydrocephalus. The damage in the brain had blocked the natural pathways that facilitated the drainage of the cerebral fluids from the brain. The fluids were accumulating in her head, exerting tremendous pressure on the brain, causing more damage and a severe headache. For eight weeks, she had suffered from this headache and we didn't know. She was admitted immediately and soon there was talk about placing a shunt in her head. A shunt is a tube that runs from her head down to her abdomen. It's attached to a pump that is placed in the brain. The pump senses the fluid pressure and releases it down through the tube to be absorbed by the body. This was not an easy surgery and I did not wish to do it at this hospital. I contacted a doctor I knew from her stay at the NICU and asked for a referral to a trustworthy neurosurgeon at NY Presbyterian. She promised to do her best. Two hours later, Stephanie and I found ourselves in a medical transfer heading to NY Presbyterian.

The neurosurgery team did not waste any time. Once we arrived, they ran another MRI to determine the severity of the swelling and the best location to place the shunt. Meanwhile, the ER team ran blood tests and we all waited for the operating room to be available. Seeing the MRI results, the team moved her to the top of the list. She was taken in within hours of arriving at the ER. The operation went well and the shunt started pumping out the extra fluids immediately. Her head began shrinking back to its normal size within days. After finishing a course of antibiotics, we were discharged from the hospital.

The shunt ended the screaming episodes, but now we had to deal with other issues. The feeding problem was not fixed. She still could not latch onto the bottle and suck efficiently. The projectile vomiting continued despite the acid reflux medications. Soon after the operation, her left leg stopped moving. One morning I noticed that she only kicked her right leg. The left one just hung in place. The doctors had no explanation for it. Just like any of her other symptoms they couldn't explain, they blamed it on the brain damage. During that period, I had a sweet Russian babysitter who came a couple of hours a day to give me a break. She insisted on trying to get the left leg to work again. Every day, she placed Stephanie in a warm bath and massaged her body, especially the left leg. She kept on assuring me that the leg would kick again. Within a few weeks, it did.

Seizures and sleep apnea were the cruelest enemies I had to deal with especially at night time. During the day, I always kept an eye on her. If I wasn't around for some reason, someone else watched her. I was terrified to leave her alone because of the fear of seizures and sleep apnea. I was always on alert. Because of this fear, I could not sleep at night. For a long time, I sat in a chair beside her crib and watched her sleep. When my eyelids and shoulders got too heavy, I would lean over the railing, stretch my arms on top of her chest and snooze for a few minutes. The countless sleep-deprived nights took a toll on my physical and emotional health.

During the first year of her life, Stephanie and I spent more time in the hospital than at home. One emergency after another kept us going back to the ER during all hours of the day. Sometimes, the ER visit lasted only a few hours. Other times we got admitted for a few days. Between my day shift and Ted's night shift, two or three weeks would pass without us being home at the same time with the children. My mom and aunt helped care for the older two children when I wasn't there.

Constant State of Emergency

Living in a state of emergency wears you down. My stress levels were very high due to the lack of sleep as well as the emotional and mental burdens. At any time, day or night, Stephanie would get sick and need to be taken to the ER. The children got used to grabbing their bags quickly, and running to the car so I could drop them off at grandma's on my way to the hospital. Other times they would wake up in the morning and not find me at home because I had run to the hospital in the middle of the night. I tried to keep life as normal as possible for them and protect them from all the emergencies. As much as I could, I kept a strong and positive front. I didn't want them to worry or resent their sister.

I relied so much on God's grace to keep me going. I can still feel the physical and emotional tiredness as I write these words. I don't know how I was able to keep up with the demands of life during that season but I know that God's hand was with me always and I am grateful. I believe I even experienced an angelic intervention at least once. I was extremely exhausted one night when Stephanie became sick and needed to be taken to the ER. It was two or three o'clock in the morning. I couldn't reach my brother to have him come stay with the children so Ted had to stay home. I secured Stephanie in her car seat, collapsed her carriage, stowed it in the back of the car, and climbed into the driver's seat. I was basically dragging myself, but she kept screaming and I knew I had to move immediately. I started the car and closed my eyes for a quick prayer. The next thing I knew, I was pulling up to the parking valet at the hospital. I do not recall the 30-minute drive. I don't have an explanation for this. Did I fall asleep and an angel drove the car? Was I so tired that I can't remember driving the car? I don't know. All I know is God was there for me every time I needed him.

> GOD WAS THERE FOR ME EVERY TIME I NEEDED HIM

CHAPTER SIX
Sleeping Beauty

I don't know how after all these years I still remember the exact day of the week one particular incident happened. Possibly because our brain vividly remembers events that are attached to intense feelings, positive or negative. Or maybe I still remember the details of this episode because it was the second time in her life that Stephanie stared death in the face and got away. It could be because Ted and I prayed with an intensity and fervor we had never felt before or since. For whatever reason, that trauma will never be erased from my memory for as long as I live.

During her younger years and due to her fragile lungs, any respiratory viruses or infections proved to complicate matters for her and endanger her life. When it came to Stephanie, there was nothing common about the common cold. It often started with a stuffy nose and rapidly progressed to a full-fledged pneumonia in record time. Where any other child could get away with sniffles and a fever, Stephanie ended up in the emergency room almost every time she caught a cold. After a few episodes of pneumonia, Kim, her nanny, and I recognized the pattern and developed a protocol to assist us in identifying the proper time to rush to the emergency room before it was too late.

Granted, we limited her exposure to other people, especially from September to April. Despite all the cautious efforts, she still got sick several times each year. At the first sign of a cold we would be on high alert and keep an eye on her breathing patterns and oxygen levels. Kim would immediately take her to see her pediatrician to rule out any infections and determine if she needed any antibiotics. We kept a nebulizer at arm's reach and we were always stocked on steroids and bronchodilator meds like Pulmicort and Xopenex. We learned to recognize the early signs of pneumonia or upper respiratory infection. She received frequent chest physical therapy which helped keep her lungs and bronchial tubes from accumulating mucus. In general, the plan was simple. First, do everything we could to prevent her from catching a cold. When that failed, we spared no effort in trying to avoid ending up in the hospital. The plan wasn't always successful and she was at the emergency room more often than we liked.

It was mid-morning on a Thursday when Kim expressed her concerns about Stephanie's breathing. She was about five years old and had been battling an ear infection the previous day. Our plan was already in motion as we gave her nebulizer treatments and monitored her breathing.

"Do the usual treatments and I will check with you in a couple of hours." I told Kim as I went on to resume homeschooling my other children.

At this point, things could go in either direction. Only time would tell.

Later that day, Kim reported, "No major changes have occurred since the morning."

"Get her suitcase ready anyway just in case we need to go to the hospital." I answered.

"It's always ready, Faye," she reminded me. Kim had a suitcase filled with all the necessities in case we had to rush to the hospital at a moment's notice.

By early evening it became obvious to me we would be spending the night at the emergency room. I called Ted at work to update him on her status.

"You sound worried," he said.

"Just frustrated. I hoped to avoid the hospital this time but it looks like she has to go," I sighed. "Please, come home early to watch the children. The sooner we leave, the better."

Two hours later Ted was home. During this time, Stephanie's breathing started to become more labored. She drew fast and shallow breaths. Her situation deteriorated faster than usual. By the time Ted came home, her lips had a tint of gray and the tips of her fingers took a while to turn pink after squeezing them.

"I'll be surprised if her oxygen level is any higher than 87%," I told Kim. "We have to rush."

I grabbed my handbag and the suitcase and headed for the van. Kim pushed Stephanie's carriage and followed suit.

As I walked toward the van, I was preparing myself for the battle ahead. I felt my adrenaline pumping and my emotions charging. I started to erect the familiar defensive wall around my heart and sharpen my attack weapons. Since her brain injury, I had become very suspicious of doctors and hospitals. I didn't trust their decisions and questioned their every action. I was no longer the naïve mom obeying anything the doctor said. Because of my mistrust, my interactions with the hospital staff were not always pleasant. I required an explanation about every test and procedure. And in some cases, I even rejected certain treatments against medical advice. Each time my objective was to get in and out of the hospital in the shortest time possible and with the least damage possible.

I unlocked the doors for Kim and went around to the driver's side. Settled behind the steering wheel, I tried to take deep breaths to calm myself down. Kim placed Stephanie in her car seat and was loading the carriage into the trunk when I heard the Holy Spirit speak to my heart.

"Do not argue with the doctors. Let them do whatever they see fit."

Immediately, my heart sank low in my chest and tears started to flow. I turned around, looked at Kim and told her what I had heard. No words were spoken for the remainder of the ride. We wept softly and prayed silently. We didn't know what, but we knew trouble was coming and we felt scared.

> WE DIDN'T KNOW WHAT, BUT WE KNEW TROUBLE WAS COMING AND WE FELT SCARED

Stephanie was a frequent patient at the emergency room. She was always welcomed by name and ushered immediately into triage and assigned a room. Kim and I knew the staff by name too, and that helped speed things up for us. That night, as we practically ran through the doors, I asked to see the attending doctor urgently. Stephanie's lips were turning grayer by the minute and I knew there was no time for formalities. The admitting nurse saw the horror in my eyes, took a look at Stephanie's face, and directed us to the first room to the right while yelling for the rest of the team to come. In all our ER visits, we had never been assigned to this room before. This room was equipped for the worst of emergencies. Before I even knew, Stephanie was transferred to the bed and connected to the monitor.

Doctors and nurses moved in a harmonious fashion. Each one busy doing their part. Her oxygen level was fluctuating between 77%-82%. They instantly put the nasal cannula on her face as they waited on the respiratory technician to come and fit her with a BPAP or even possibly intubate her for the ventilator. Meanwhile, I stood in the corner in silence and watched what was happening. I bit my lips a few times to keep myself from yelling. Staying out of their business was harder that I thought. One of the nurses tried to draw blood as another intern searched her body for a good vein to start an IV line. Unfortunately, Stephanie has shallow, spidery veins which makes it hard for the doctors to get an IV going. After a few failed attempts, I couldn't keep my mouth shut and I ordered them to stop and call someone from the Neonatal Intensive Care Unit. Those nurses were used to dealing with premature babies and were the only ones who are typically successful in finding a viable vein. Faced with their failed attempts and to avoid a confrontation with me, they agreed to call a nurse from the NICU.

Stephanie's oxygen levels were not improving. They switched the nasal cannula to a BPAP hoping it would do the trick. This only made matters worse. The oxygen filled her stomach with air. The face mask covered her mouth and nose. Because of the pressure against her airway, it was impossible for her to clear her throat of phlegm. She aspirated the phlegm into her lungs.

Meanwhile, the X-ray technician walked in the room with a portable X-ray machine. Everyone had to evacuate the room as he took X-ray images of her lungs. I wore the lead apron and stayed in the room to help him situate her correctly and hold her still. This was over quickly and the medical team filled the room again. Two medical students kept me occupied giving them a brief summary of her medical history. Then they wanted a detailed account of the past two days. Meanwhile, the NICU nurse was able to establish an IV line and draw blood. I took a sigh of relief as she sent the blood sample to the lab. Watching them repeatedly poke her little body to find a vein was always difficult for me.

My relief lasted only a few seconds. In came another nurse with a kit in her hand. I immediately recognized the bag and knew what was coming next. They needed a urine sample to test. Stephanie wore a diaper and could not pee in a cup. They had to insert a catheter into her bladder to obtain uncontaminated urine for reliable results. I absolutely hated the violation of privacy and the discomfort of this procedure. She was already in pain. Cold sweat covered her naked body due to the labored breathing. Wires were sticking out of her torso. Small bruises dotted her arms and legs from all the needles. And now this! What killed me the most was the fact she suffered silently. I had to be brave. I could not let her see me break down. So, I wiped my tears, forced a smile on my face and approached the bed. I held her as close as I could, covered her face with my body and started singing her favorite song as they placed the catheter in.

"There are days when I feel the best of me is ready to begin, and there are days when I feel I'm letting go and soaring on the wind. 'Cause I've learned in laughter and in pain how to survive. I get on my knees. There I am before the love that changes me. I don't know how, but there's power when I'm on my knees."

I was thankful when this part was over. The commotion in the room quieted down and the doctors left us to go check on other patients. Now we waited on tests results to come back. She struggled to keep her oxygen level above 88% even with the aid of the BPAP. Kim stayed by her side as I looked for the attending doctor to express my concerns about her blood oxygen level. She listened to me as we walked back to the room.

"We were hoping to avoid it but it seems she needs to be on the ventilator after all. You are familiar with the procedure, right?"

She was asking if I knew about the sedation part. Usually the doctors use sedating drugs to place the patient in a medical coma to prevent them from moving. Patient movement increases the risk of the breathing tube extending into their lungs.

"Unfortunately, I am familiar with it, doctor." I replied.

She tweaked with the oxygen settings for a minute and left to check for an available bed in the Pediatric Intensive Care Unit. Stephanie was transferred to the sixth floor, another place we were too familiar with. The PICU team got busy preparing her for the ventilator. They started one more IV line and an A-line. Kim and I stood against the wall watching the nurses, interns, and medical students move around the bed as if in a choreographed dance.

They called us over to kiss her before they administered the drugs to put her to sleep. It was well after midnight when things calmed down and Kim and I were left alone by her side. Kim cleaned the bed from plastic bags and cotton swabs left behind by the doctors. She then took out Stephanie's blanket and stuffed elephant and placed them on the bed. Kim always cared about making Stephanie feel comfortable and secure—especially in the hospital.

Soon the attending doctor (I will call him Dr. C.) informed us X-rays showed she had pneumonia. The lower right lobe of her lung was collapsing and a few pockets of mucus were spread around her lungs. They added a strong antibiotic to the cocktail of drugs they were already giving her.

Stephanie remained in the PICU for five weeks. Her health deteriorated from bad to worse. Her lungs were filling with fluids faster than the medical team could drain them. They inserted a plastic tube in her right side through the rib cage and into the lungs to drain the fluids out. Her kidneys and lymphatic system could not keep up with expelling the fluids. As a result, her body started to swell and her enlarged tongue protruded out of her mouth. Her heart was getting weaker as her blood oxygen levels plummeted and carbon dioxide levels soared. I was told if her heart stopped at this point, resuscitation would fail due to the high levels of carbon dioxide in her blood.

Every day, we longed for some good news or a sign of improvement. Instead, she kept getting worse. They monitored her oxygen and carbon dioxide ratios closely, took regular X-ray images of her lungs and tweaked with the settings on the ventilator.

Nothing was working. To make matters worse, her lungs were giving up. One night the ventilator got over-heated. Fumes shot out of the machine. Kim freaked out and yelled to the nurse to come. Thankfully, the PICU had another ventilator on standby and they replaced the damaged machine immediately.

Even with the help of the ventilator, her lungs were getting tired and on the verge of collapsing. The team was getting frustrated and decided to switch her from the current ventilator to a high frequency oscillatory ventilation machine. We called it the Oscillator. It supplied oxygen and a constant distending pressure to keep the lungs inflated. Her small body trembled as the machine propelled the oxygen into her chest.

Her chances of surviving this were getting slimmer by the hour. The doctors had no more tricks up their sleeve. The oscillator was their last attempt at reversing her condition. Relatives and friends joined our family in praying for her recovery. As negative reports streamed in, Ted and I found ourselves on our knees crying out for a miracle on her behalf. The PICU became a dreadful place to be as I tried to keep my faith and hope afloat. Towards the end of the third week, every time I visited her, Dr. C. reminded me to say my good byes.

> I WAS STILL HOLDING ON TO THE PROMISE I HEARD A FEW YEARS BEFORE

"She might not make it through the night," he would say.

I was shocked the first time he told me that. Then I heard the same statement from her neurologist who came to check on her from time to time. Some of my friends and relatives joined in and were encouraging me to let her go. Even though reality supported their predictions, I couldn't bring myself to let her go. I was still holding on to the promise I heard a few years before. Ted and I pressed into God and spent sleepless nights in prayer interceding for her. I was not ready to admit defeat yet. Soon enough I became annoyed and slightly angry any time the doctor hinted at the possibility of her approaching death.

The first ray of hope came when a friend of mine called out of the blue.

"You've been on my mind and in my prayers for a few days. What's going on?" She said.

"Stephanie's in the hospital. She's not doing well," I cried.

"This explains the dream I had last night! I saw Stephanie lying in a hospital bed. The word 'death' was stamped on her forehead. I saw you holding on to her, determined not to let go."

She gave me a minute to process her words, then continued, "She'll pull through, Faye. Don't doubt it."

I felt some peace and calm after she hung up. My prayers were being heard. The next day I went to the hospital with renewed hope.

It wasn't long before Dr. C. came to check on her. There were no changes in her condition. As soon as he finished reading her chart, he asked me to step outside into the corridor and proceeded to impress on me the urgency of her deteriorated state. This time I didn't silently agree with his statements.

I motioned for him to stop talking.

I gathered my courage, took a deep breath and said, "I listened to you say this to me a few times already. I respect you and respect his hospital. I chose to come here because I trust in the education and experience of the medical team. Please remember that you and everyone on this team is working for my daughter. Your main objective is to make her well. So, you should use every tool you have to keep my daughter alive. I thank you for all your efforts, but the last time I checked you were not God and you don't get to decide when she gets to die."

I walked away from him.

Time to Act

After my earlier phone conversation with my friend and the confrontation I just had with Dr. C., I decided to act upon my faith. In my heart, I had faith that Stephanie would conquer this state and come home to us. But I wanted my words and actions to align with my belief. I decided to celebrate her recovery as if it had already happened.

The next day I passed by the bakery on my way to the hospital and purchased a box of their best cookies. I placed the box in the doctors' lounge with a note that said, "Celebrating Stephanie's recovery." I also had a box of chocolates by her bed and offered a piece to each person who came to visit her. The staff must've thought I had lost my mind from all the pressure. I was so full of assurance and busy fighting the battle in the unseen realm that I could care less about my image or what people thought of me.

Soon Dr. C.'s rotation ended and a new attending doctor joined the staff. Dr. P. seemed a bit more optimistic and was open to some of the team's suggestions regarding changes in her treatment plan. For many days, Kim had been trying to convince the intern in charge of Stephanie's case (Dr. B.) to change the settings on the ventilation to allow her some control over her breathing. Even though Dr. B was sympathetic and willing to try, he was unable to persuade Dr. C. to sign off on it. The opportunity presented itself again when Dr. P. came on board. He agreed to give it a try. It was a risky move, a sort of a hail Mary. After all, she was dying. What worse could happen?

Nothing worse happened. Actually, Kim was right all along. Stephanie needed to be in control. As soon as they gave her some control, her lungs kicked in and started breathing on their own. Dr. B. kept a close eye on her progress. For a few days, I watched in awe as Dr. B. interacted with Stephanie with a skill I hadn't seen in a doctor for a long time. He abandoned science, facts, and his ego and communicated with her through intuition. He connected to her soul—an artful skill that is almost nonexistent among doctors these days. Stephanie, still in a coma, and Dr. B. engaged in a brilliant nonverbal conversation as he allowed her body to take the lead. He listened to her hints and adjusted the settings on the machine and the dosage of the sedating drugs accordingly. Other than a couple of times where she became too tired to breathe, he was on cue the whole time. What Dr. B. did was nothing short of a miracle. We are forever in his debt.

I was buying groceries for the house when Kim called.

"She's awake. Get down here."

I left the basket on the floor, got in my car, and drove down to the City. She was already extubated when I arrived. I cried when I saw her smile at me. We had to wait for two more days for observation and final tests before we could leave.

Finally, after 35 long days, the nightmare was over. We packed her belongings, secured her in the stroller and headed out the PICU. Turning a corner in the hallway, I saw Dr. C. walking towards us. I stood for a moment, locked eyes with him, and continued walking. Was that an embarrassed look that I saw on his face?

FINALLY, AFTER 35 LONG DAYS,
THE NIGHTMARE WAS OVER

CHAPTER SEVEN

Why?

> "THE WHY QUESTION IS A VICTIM QUESTION;
> AND YOU ARE NOT A VICTIM."
>
> *—Graham Cooke*

As parents and individuals who care for a child with special needs, we have asked ourselves and God, "Why?" many times. We've asked it in secret and out loud. We have worried over it in our minds. We found ourselves trying to make sense of the tragic event and the pain associated with it.

It is human to want to blame someone or something for the misfortunes that afflict us. Most of the time we end up blaming ourselves, God, or both.

I have gone through this cycle of blame many times in the past 18 years. For a long time, I could not come to peace with the fact I lost one daughter and the other one was suffering on a daily basis. I needed to know why!

It was easy to feel guilty. I wanted to punish someone for this horrible incident and I decided it would be me. Condemning thoughts were always playing in the background and I could not escape them.

"It must've been my trip to Israel that caused me to have premature labor," I told myself.

"What if I missed the signs because I wasn't paying attention to my body?"

The idea that I, as a mother, had done something to ruin the lives of my twins tortured me. Because I harbored these thoughts in my mind, it caused me to feel like everyone else was blaming me too. In fact, some people did attribute the misfortunate events to a faulty walk with God, and they told me so.

Immediately after the death of Deborah, friends and family members called and visited. They wanted to check on me and try to bring comfort to my heart. Some were a tremendous help and brought hope with encouraging words. Others, however, were prompting me to check the intentions of my heart.

"You must've done something wrong to displease God. That is why He is punishing you," said one.

"Just because you're blessed financially, doesn't mean that God is pleased with you," said another.

Thankfully, my mom realized what effect this was having on me and quickly intervened. She strongly suggested I not answer the phone for a while, and started screening the calls before she would let me speak to the caller.

More than once I heard her say, "Faye is busy right now. She'll get back to you later."

I am so grateful for her wisdom. I definitely did not want to believe God was punishing me for my sins. Sadly, I did not have a biblical understanding at the time, but I thought God was a nice person and He would not punish me through my children. This belief carried me through for a while until I was able to prove from the Bible that God would never do this to anyone.

I am not a theologian or a five-fold Bible teacher. I am expressing my beliefs and the knowledge I have gained from listening to trustworthy teachers, reading many books, studying my Bible, asking many questions, and conversing with the Holy Spirit. The conclusion I came to took me years to research and implement in my life. As I mentioned earlier, I did not have a sound biblical perspective to protect me from battling with shame, guilt, and blame. I had simple trust and faith that He was better than what my friends said. Nevertheless, this was not enough because at times I did question Him, especially when things became really tough. Feelings are nice, but they will not stand in the face of adversity. Only the truth will carry us through and bring us to victory.

> **FEELINGS ARE NICE, BUT THEY WILL NOT STAND IN THE FACE OF ADVERSITY**

Essentially, God had to correct the way I viewed Him. In the first few months of dealing with the disappointment of the death of Deborah and the hospitalization of Stephanie, He asked me to trust Him to do two things on a daily basis. Each morning before I faced the day, I was to stand in front of a mirror and repeat this phrase to myself: "God is good today even if I don't understand. The devil will not win because I have the victory."

In the beginning I just repeated the words out of obedience, but later on I noticed I started to believe what I said. I found myself repeating it out loud to myself and others every time I found myself in a corner.

The second thing He asked me to do was to write this sentence on a 3x5 card and read it when I needed to. It said, "I will let neither people nor circumstances dictate the quality of my life. God has a destiny for me and I will accomplish it." Soon enough that concept became an integral part of my thought pattern. Now I look back at the simple phrases and realize how powerful they were. The first one declared who He was and the second one stated my identity. I realized that our circumstances are all about who we're becoming (Graham Cooke).

I don't interpret God, His character, or motives through my circumstance. Doing so results in having a distorted image of who God is and how He feels about me. It also results in asking a lot of why questions that don't have satisfying answers. Because our circumstances change all the time, our view of who God is will fluctuate accordingly. We will end up believing in a schizophrenic God. This opens the door to doubt, fear, and disbelief. It shakes our relationship with God.

On the contrary, I view my circumstances through God's character. I look for God in my circumstances because He said He will never leave or forsake me (Deuteronomy 31:6). This leads me to ask better questions like, what, how and where. So instead of asking, "Why are you (God) doing this to me? Why does my child have to endure all this pain? Why does my family have to go through this?" I ask, "How are you (God) going to take this tough situation and turn it into something beautiful for me and my family? How are you going to use it to shape me and make me more like Jesus? How is this going to strengthen my faith and trust in you? How is this building my character and reputation?"

Basically what I am asking is, "What does this mean? What shall I do about it?" (Acts 2:12; 2:37). "What does this situation mean to my identity and to our relationship? What must I do in the light of what you (God) want to do?" Instead of focusing on the unresolved problem which lead to unfruitful questions, I focus on my relationship with Father God. This leads to maturity on my end and more intimacy with Him.

Today, I am at total peace with my daughter's condition. I am, nevertheless, declaring and believing for her healing. But the fact that God loves me so much and her being disabled does not confuse me or trouble me at all. It took me years to come to this place of rest. Because I know how it feels to be on the other side, I want you to experience the peace I have and put to rest all fears, doubts, guilt and shame. In order to reach this place, I had to change my perspective of God and myself. In the coming pages allow me to share with you the insights that brought me to have peace with God and stop blaming Him or myself for life's trials.

Concept #1 – God is a Good God

This might not sound like a new revelation. Even though we have been repeating the phrase, "God is good all the time, and all the time God is good," in reality we have been blaming Him for doing bad things—all the time. How can we believe that He is good and also believe that He is able to bestow sickness on us? God is good because his nature is good. He is made out of goodness. There is no evil in Him and therefore, He is unable to grant us evil things. One can only bequeath what one owns and since He is made out of peace, harmony, health, love, joy, etc., He can't impart sickness, death, rape, war, etc. He is the source of all good gifts (James 1:17). God is in the business of doing good. That is why He says that He will cause all things to work together for our good (Romans 8:28). His intentions and thoughts towards us are ones of prosperity and blessings (Jeremiah 29:11).

The Bible is clear about who is the source of evil: "The thief's purpose is to steal and kill and destroy. My purpose is to give them a rich and satisfying life" (John 10:10). Can it be any clearer than this? Sometimes we credit God with questionable actions when in fact He is innocent from such accusations. Somewhere along the way, the church even agreed with and taught that sickness was acceptable because God has a divine purpose behind everything He does. The notion we are to humbly and thankfully accept sickness as if it's a blessing in disguise, makes me furious. That God, as a parent, uses sickness and pain to teach us important life lessons and to help us mature as Christians is another idea that makes me nauseated. Parents who break their child's arm as a means of discipline or teaching tool are termed abusers. They are prosecuted and punished for their actions. How then can we entertain the idea of a loving, good God utilizing evil as a parenting tool? For a long time I was confused about this. When I finally understood God was not the source of pain and destruction, I was able to conclude God was not responsible for the death of Deborah or for Stephanie's brain damage. Instead my heart now echoes David's words, "For the Lord is good. His unfailing love continues forever, and His faithfulness continues to each generation" (Psalm 100:1).

Concept #2 – God's Sovereignty Vs. My Responsibility

Sovereign and "in control" appear to mean the same thing and are sometimes used interchangeably. This may cause a lot of confusion when it comes to God's authority in the world. The Merriam-Webster dictionary defines sovereign as "an acknowledged leader." I like that. God is the leader. He is the King of kings and the Lord of lords. On the other hand, it defines "in control" as "to have power over" or "to exercise restraining or directing influence over." Just because He is the leader doesn't mean He controls every action or event that takes place on this earth. This might be a bit hard to accept. It was difficult for me to come to terms with the fact God is not in total control of this world. After all, He is the all-mighty, all-knowing God. It is true that He has the ability to control everything but He chose not to. He chose to give us freedom over our choices from the very beginning.

Let's unpack this thought a little bit. God created Adam and Eve in His own image which included having freedom of choice. Why would God take this risk? Because without freedom of choice there couldn't be real loving relationships. It would have been easier for God to influence them to obey Him and not eat from the forbidden tree. It could've saved Jesus from dying on the cross and we would all be living in the Garden now. But the whole thing would be fake. God wanted us to be aware of all our options. This way, every time a person chooses Him over everything else, it would be because of love and real commitment. He loves us so much that He respects our decisions even if they break His heart sometimes.

To believe God is in control and exerts that control over both man and nature may seem like a comforting idea, but it's not. I can find at least two faults in it. First, it makes God responsible for every inhumane and cruel action ever made. That means God gets to choose who gets raped, sold to slavery, or murdered. It also implies God wills people to suffer from hideous diseases like AIDS and cancer. How about all the babies that are born with genetic disorders or lifelong sickness? How does God choose who gets the bad fortune? Does He have a list of who's naughty or nice? Does He check it twice?

Second, this idea absolves humans from any responsibility. If we don't have a choice over our actions, then we can't claim credit for accomplishing anything. Neither will we get punished for faulty behavior. Imagine with me a world where you have no say in anything. You are preprogrammed to be a certain type of person. You'd be lucky if you were selected to be a successful businessman, for example, and not a serial killer. Imagine you discovered the cure for a rare disease, but no one acknowledges your effort because it was God that caused you to do it. It had nothing to do with you after all. What if your neighbor was chosen to be a rapist or a serial killer and no one can lock him up because it's not his fault? He's just playing whatever role God desired for him. Do you realize the absurdness of the idea that God is in control of everything that happens on this earth?

One could write a book about this topic alone. Indeed, there are more qualified authors that have written good books exploring this subject in more depth. My point here is even though God is sovereign, He chooses not to be in control of us. We have the freedom of choice, given to us by Him. We make our own decisions and these decisions affect us and the people around us. This is called the law of sowing and reaping (Galatians 6:7). We need to stop blaming God for all the tragic events in our lives. We must take responsibility for our own actions. Sometimes, bad things happen because we make bad choices (James 1:13-16). For example, people who have liver disease because of a lifestyle of excessive alcohol consumption or drug abuse have only themselves to blame.

The sad reality is the law of sowing and reaping extends beyond the person who is sowing. In most cases, the decisions we make affect other people—mainly the ones closest to us. Children suffer the result of their parents' parenting skills or lack thereof. In Stephanie's case, her brain damage happened in part because of a faulty medical practice of vaccinating immature, under-weight babies. Even if it wasn't intentional, it still altered our lives forever. She also suffered—and continues to suffer—because the ER attending doctor decided to dismiss my concerns and send me home without physically checking her. If he had, she would have been placed on antibiotics in time. We are reaping the aftermath of his mistaken choice.

Concept #3 – We Live in a Fallen World

Sickness, death, and tragic events sometimes happen simply because we live in a broken world. Sin entered our lives and our world when Adam and Eve relinquished their God-given authority over to Satan. They were given total dominion over the earth and were to rule it with love, harmony, and care. They gave that right up when they chose to trust and believe in Satan's lies. Sin and death were then introduced to our lives. Jesus claimed back the authority and dispensed it to His body, the church. However, until we fully walk in our identity as sons and daughters and take charge of this dominion, the world will stay under the influence of evil (Romans 8:19-22).

Concept #4 – Demonic Influence Affects the Natural World

I also believe that some tragic conditions and diseases exist because of actual evil demonic influence like demonic possessions or oppression. I'm not an expert in this area and will not attempt to sound like one. I've seen and heard of cases where people were instantly healed after a demonic spirit was cast out of their bodies. Look up the story of the demon-possessed man in Luke 8:26-39, and the dumb man in Matthew 9:32-34. I don't believe this is the case for my daughter, but I do believe that some physical conditions are the result of demonic spiritual influence.

In conclusion, I believe that God is good to us all the time. He is my awesome Daddy. He wants the best for me and gives me good gifts because He is made out of goodness. I believe bad things happen for one of these four reasons:

- We make bad choices
- We are affected by other people's wrong or bad choices
- We live in a fallen, broken world
- Because of a direct demonic influence

I also believe that we have the authority in the name of Jesus to change the world, to heal the sick and to raise the dead. It is our responsibility and privilege to alter the reality of this world from death to life and from pain to joy.

> I DO NOT VIEW GOD'S CHARACTER THROUGH MY CIRCUMSTANCES—RATHER, I VIEW MY CIRCUMSTANCES THROUGH GOD'S CHARACTER

CHAPTER EIGHT

Heart to Heart

Mothering or caring for a special-needs child is not fundamentally different than mothering any other child. It does, however, intensify the experience. Every mother faces and struggles with her weaknesses on a daily basis. She regularly battles with fear, doubt, and guilty thoughts of inadequacy. She wonders if she's doing a good job caring for her children. Because she cares and loves them so much, she wants to make sure she is doing her best in everything. I don't want to depreciate the role of any mother. In fact, I wish to honor and bless all parents for the sacrifices they make and their efforts to raise the next generation. Having said that, mothers with special needs children face some difficulties unique to their situation. In the following pages, I will share my heart and be transparent about the struggles I have faced in caring for Stephanie for the past 18 years. I hope my experience will encourage some of you to realize you are not alone.

Helplessness

Perhaps the most difficult feeling I've struggled with was helplessness. I wish I could say I am totally over this. I am not. I can say, though, I struggle with it less and less as I mature. When I speak of feeling helpless, I'm talking about my child's suffering and not being able to alleviate the pain. I am talking about watching her trapped inside her body, praying to God for healing without an answer as of this day, and wishing I could carry her pain and disability so she could be free. All this has added to my frustration and feeling of helplessness. No amount of money, time or energy can fix her situation. I stretched myself in every direction, yet nothing helped. Frustration and helplessness were a constant battlefield for me. I wanted to fix things. I wanted to fix her. I hit my head against this wall on a daily basis.

I could not and would not accept this was her fate. No way! Not on my watch. I was determined she was going to walk and I was going to make it happen one way or another. In my efforts to fight helplessness, I made a lot of decisions. Some of which I regretted later on and some, I was glad I made. Now, there is nothing wrong about trying to make her life better or wanting her to be healed. It's the motive behind it and the power that fueled it that drove me to my wit's end. I was driven by frustration and helplessness.

> **HOW DO YOU HELP YOUR CHILD WHEN THERE IS NO ANSWER TO HER PROBLEM?**

I hated feeling helpless and needed to do something about it. There's no worse feeling than watching a loved one suffer while you can't do anything to help, not because you are not willing but rather because you are incapable. What can you do in the face of a damaged brain? How can you fix that? Even the most advanced medical technologies can't fix it. How can you help your child when there's no answer to her problem? Helplessness and frustration closed on me like a noose suffocating the life out of me. I had to be honest with myself about why I felt helpless and frustrated before I could get rid of the noose around my neck.

Allow me to share with you some of the things in my own heart that have contributed to feeling helpless and being driven by this feeling.

1. Pride

Pride was one of three hidden factors that empowered my frustration and helplessness. I thought I was too good to have a child that was not "normal." These things happen to other people, but not to me. I didn't deserve this. This might communicate the wrong message about who I was. For example, people might think I had done something wrong to deserve this problem. How can I call myself a woman of faith and have a child that is sick? Pride would not allow me to accept the situation.

2. Control

Control was the second factor. I am a perfectionist and this was not a perfect situation, so it must be contained and controlled. Frustration was the natural outcome of my efforts to control Stephanie's health challenges. I have a need for things to be in order and she was definitely out of order. Being unable to control aspects of this challenge led me to exert a crazy amount of control in other areas. I grew out of balance and out of equilibrium and this created great frustration for me as well as for those who loved me and were close enough to be affected by my constant striving to regain control of what was totally uncontrollable.

3. Fear

The third factor was fear. I was afraid to accept Stephanie as she is because I thought this meant two things I did not want to face. First, I don't have enough faith to heal her, and second, God is not willing to heal her. I struggled with fear for years before I realized these were lies which had no foundation. Until I understood God's perspective on Stephanie's disability I was not able to be free. These three factors were hidden deep inside my heart. They were not the subject of everyday meditation. Still, they drove almost all my decisions and how I felt about and treated not only Stephanie but my other children.

Fighting Helplessness With Activity

In my attempt to fix Stephanie I took her to see many doctors, specialists, therapists and healers. I traveled many miles, spent countless hours and a lot of money to find some sort of relief for her. When traditional medicine fell short, I looked for alternative measures in the natural healing arena. We took her to see brain development specialists. We followed a strict schedule of therapies and diets in an attempt to reverse the brain damage. We tried countless supplements and herbs to stop seizures and build new neuro connections in the brain. We purchased a Hyperbaric Oxygen Chamber to saturate her brain cells with oxygen. Chiropractic care was and still is a part of her life. Some of these treatments were a waste of time, money and effort. Some delivered limited relief or small breakthroughs that kept our hope and faith alive.

When the time came I also decided to homeschool Stephanie. I chose not to send her to a school for special needs children. I did not trust anyone with her. Doing so forced me to learn to do all the therapies that she needed. I then taught them to her nanny who worked on her daily. The other decision I took was to study Naturopathy. I formally studied Naturopathy and other therapies in order to help her. If it wasn't for my drive to fix her, I would have chosen another field to study. I can't tell you what our life would have been if we took different paths, but I know feeling helpless or frustrated is not a good foundation for making life decisions.

Thankfully, after a few years I was healed from hopelessness. As I understood how God felt about Stephanie and His expectations from me, I was free from frustration. I admitted and faced my pride. I repented and humbled myself. When I realized how much God loved me, I was able to let go of control and trust in His timing for her healing. The knowledge I gained from studying His Word combined with letting go of my need to fix her empowered me. I realized I am more powerful and able to help her than I took credit for. God helped me recognize the difference between the issues I can fix and the ones I can't. Little by little I started to trust Him with the problems that were out of my control and celebrate the small victories.

> I STARTED TO TRUST GOD WITH THE PROBLEMS THAT WERE OUT OF MY CONTROL AND CELEBRATE SMALL VICTORIES

I could never heal her brain, but I can help her control the seizures. At one point Stephanie was on three different seizure medications. Not only did they not stop the seizures, they caused her to be drugged and not aware of her surroundings. When she seized we also administered a suppository called Diastat to stop the seizure. This numbed her nerves and relaxed all her muscles. Sometimes it also relaxed her lungs and made it hard for her to breathe. Other times the Diastat was not effective enough and we had to drive her to the emergency room for different meds to be administered. After many ER runs and a few incidents with collapsed lungs, I fought to take her off the medications. It was awhile before I could convince her neurologist that she was better off without them. Then it took 18 months to gradually taper her off the medications.

Stephanie still gets seizures, but she is no longer numb or drugged. She no longer suffers from the medications' side effects. We are able to stop the seizures with prayer and acupressure point techniques. Helplessness and frustration no more rule my life.

Recently, an incident happened that tested me in this area. Kim was taking Stephanie to see the chiropractor when Stephanie was attacked by a dog in front of our house. I was working in my room when my oldest daughter started yelling, "Mom, come down. Stephanie was bit by a dog." At first, I thought it was a joke. *No way this actually happened,* I told myself.

Sure enough, I hurried to the street and I saw Kim pressing a cloth against Stephanie's head. Amongst the sobs and tears she told me the dog came charging at her without any warning. Speechless, the dog's owner held the leash and stood in shame by the side of the house. This was our neighbor's dog, a man we had known for three years. He was walking down the block when the dog decided to attack Stephanie. She was sitting in her carriage waiting for Kim to transfer her into the carseat when the dog jumped from behind and bit her head. He peeled the skin off her scalp before Kim was able to scare him away.

The paramedics and the police escorted us to the hospital where she got nine stitches to repair the damage. Naturally, I felt shock, fear, and anger. I had to immediately make a decision to forgive our neighbor for not controlling his dog. I did not want any resentment to take hold of my heart. The surprise came the next day. I was till processing the event and all of a sudden, the feeling of helplessness crept up on me and I was overtaken by it. I nursed it for a day before I reminded myself that I overcame this a long time ago and should not give in to it anymore.

My point is this: just because you are healed from a bad experience doesn't mean you will not be tempted to act like you are still in bondage. You need to remember and live out your freedom as you face situations that might take you down a painful path.

Guilt

The other emotion I struggled with was guilt. For a long long time, guilt was my companion. Like a close friend, it never left my side. I felt it, thought about it, and let it guide my actions too. It weighed my heart down and robbed me of my joy and peace. On countless nights, I found myself unsuccessfully chasing after sleep because of guilt. No matter how much I tried to convince myself I was not responsible for Stephanie's illness, I still felt it was somehow my fault.

Guilt is almost always accompanied by shame. They are a powerful duo that paralyze and cripple your potential. Guilt escorted every decision I made regarding her care. I always questioned myself and my ability to care for her. No matter what decision I made, I felt guilty about it. I felt guilty about not carrying the twins to terms. I felt guilty about not being there when Deborah died. I felt guilty for hiring someone to help me care for Stephanie. I felt guilty for leaving my other children home to be with her in the hospital. I felt guilty about leaving her in the hospital and going home to check on the other children. Guilt engulfed me.

For me, guilt was the toughest issue to deal with. It was a weak area in my life even before the twins were born. It originated from my culture and the way I was brought up as a woman. Feelings of guilt came as a result of false expectations and lies that I believed in. As the Holy Spirit opened my mind to understand the root causes of my guilt, I became aware that I could let go of these expectations and be free from the guilt. It was easier said than done. I battled with guilt for years before I was able to be completely untangled. It had its vicious fangs deeply hooked in me. But again, through surrender and supernatural grace, I was set free.

Forgiveness

Going through a traumatic experience like the one I endured, creates floods of highly charged emotions, both negative and positive. It exposes you to unusual scenarios and makes you vulnerable. Trauma tests your character and unmasks your weaknesses. I had to deal with and navigate through many emotions like grief, shock, and anger over the death of Deborah. For a few years I did not have the time or the capacity to process many emotions. I just stuffed them down or pushed them to the side. I tagged them with a mental note that said "process at a later time." Father God gave me grace to handle the difficult circumstances before me without being entangled with the complicated emotions. As time passed and Stephanie's emergencies subsided, I attended to those emotions and sought healing for my wounded heart.

The one thing that God did not allow me to push to the side, however, was offense. He made me deal with it either immediately or shortly after it happened. I am a forgiving person, and up until that time I never had a hard time forgiving people. At the same time, I had never experienced offenses at this level of intensity or frequency before. Nevertheless, the Holy Spirit convicted my heart to forgive no matter how painful the offense was. He knew I would not have been able to sustain myself through it all while harboring unforgiveness in my heart. He made it clear from day one that forgiveness was mandatory in order for me to be at peace and operate in grace. Forgiveness was also vital for continuing to lead worship which I did during that time.

I tried to get away with it at first; partly because I was too tired to deal with wounds and emotions, and partly because I wasn't sure that whoever offended me deserved to be forgiven. I wanted to blame someone for my pain. How can I forgive the doctor that denied my daughter timely treatment and in turn ruined her life? How can I forgive myself for trusting him and not insisting on staying in the ER? But soon enough I learned that unforgiveness was hurting me and prohibiting me from living a peaceful life. I will not discuss the doctrine of forgiveness here, but I will share what helped me to take that step.

God revealed to me how much He loved me and forgave me. He did not hold me responsible for what happened to Stephanie. And if God, who is the judge of all creation, decides I am free and forgiven, then who am I to not forgive myself? The same goes for any person that offended me. God is the one and only judge. It is not my place to withhold forgiveness from anyone. I will not compromise my peace and freedom by holding people hostage in my resentment cage. With the help of the Holy Spirit, I was able to open the prison door open and release those who offended me.

Support is Vital

I want to take a minute to give tribute to the community of people that supported us throughout the years. I can't imagine my life without these people. I am a very independent woman. Asking for help is not easy for me. However, going through a journey like this one without the love and support of family and friends would have been impossible. I am thankful for all the people who prayed for us and believed with us. We are made to live and function within a community and never to be alone. Be grateful for and accept the kindness of the people around you. Ask for their help. Most of my friends wanted to pray for us, babysit our children, and cook for us. I wasn't wise and humble enough to accept their kindness as often as I should. It would have been a much more pleasant journey if I had.

If there is one piece of advice I can give you it would be this: allow people into your life. Do not hide away. It is okay for your friends to see you in your weak moments. Humility and transparency do not make you weak, on the contrary, it shows strength. Be true to what is going on. Embrace the situation and allow others to carry you when your legs become weary.

LEARN TO ACCEPT AND EMBRACE
HELP FROM OTHERS—YOU
NEED NOT WALK ALONE

CHAPTER NINE
Therapies

I desire to share with you our experiences with some medications and therapies. My intention is not to give medical advice nor to belittle any method of treatment. My hope is to encourage you as you look for answers to the ailments of those you love. Perhaps our experiences will help you avoid some pitfalls or open your mind to alternative possibilities. I acknowledge that every child reacts differently to supplements and medications. I'm only sharing Stephanie's results in the hopes our experiences may help someone else. Let's proceed with this thought in mind.

Vaccines

I couldn't write this book without addressing the big elephant in the room. Vaccination is a hot and controversial topic. I'd be a fool to try and convince you to take my side on this issue, because I don't have the background to offer you a scientific proof that vaccines are detrimental to children's health. Scientists, educators, and medical doctors have been debating this subject for years. Each camp presents a compelling argument with research and theories to back them up. I understand the fear associated with having an epidemic outbreak of disease. But I can't ignore the increase of neurological and behavioral disorders cases allegedly associated with vaccinations. Stephanie was not born with brain damage. All her tests—which included an MRI of her brain prior to her vaccinations—showed normal results. The doctors predicted some physical developmental delays because of her early birth and low birth weight. Actual physical damage to the brain happened in the wake of the group B meningitis infection.

A day or two before she was released from the NICU, she was inoculated with a variety of vaccinations including the meningitis vaccine. Two weeks later she came down with meningitis. Was that a coincidence? Or was her immune system too weak to handle the strain of meningitis in the vaccine? The CDC states that one in a million people have severe reactions to the vaccine. Was she that one child? How about the DTaP vaccine? One side effect is permanent brain damage. The CDC doesn't state how often that occurs. To the FDA or the CDC, these severe cases are statistics and numbers—rare and tolerable. Maybe the sacrifice of one child is justified by the benefit to so many other children. But these cases are not just statistics on a chart somewhere. These cases are our children.

In my heart, no benefit can justify robbing a child of the chance to be who they were meant to be. These cases are children that might never walk, talk, hear, or see. These are children who were not allowed to contribute beauty and potential to our world. Unfortunately, I didn't make the connection between vaccination and her brain damage soon enough. Stephanie experienced seizure activity associated with the meningitis. She was immediately treated with Phenobarbital and continued to take it for at least two months after the incident as a preventative measure. However, the doctor weaned her off Phenobarbital and she was seizure free for at least eight to ten months. Then in the spring of 2001, she was given the chicken pox vaccine (Varicella) and within 24 hours, the seizures returned and have not stopped since. Coincidence? I will let you decide.

One more story about vaccines before I move on to another topic. Premature babies born at 35 weeks or earlier are given the Synagis shot during RSV season. Even though it's not considered a vaccine, Synagis is an FDA-approved prescription injection of antibodies. It's given monthly to protect high-risk babies from respiratory syncytial virus or RSV for short. At first, I didn't tie it together. It took a few shots for me to confirm a relationship between the timing of the shot and the flu episodes. Every month, within days of taking the shot, Stephanie would come down with severe cold symptoms that sometimes turned into pneumonia. Needless to say, I stopped giving her the shots as soon as I made the connection.

In the aftermath of all of that, I stopped giving my children vaccinations. Again, I'm only sharing our story. Whether to vaccinate or not is a personal decision and should be approached seriously. Do your research. Ask all the questions. Read the warnings. Make an educated decision. I pray that no child suffers the way my daughter has.

Seizures

As I mentioned earlier, our introduction to seizures occurred during the meningitis infection. It lasted for a couple of days and was addressed by administering Phenobarbital, an anti-seizure medication. For months after the initial seizure, I was terrified of it happening again and I couldn't leave her alone for a minute. I had trouble sleeping at night for fear of her seizing again. Thankfully, I didn't have to deal with seizures for about a year following the brain damage trauma. As I mentioned earlier, right after she was inoculated with the chicken pox vaccine, she started having seizures again on a daily basis. You can never get used to seizures. It hurts every time just as much. Seizures are versatile. They could manifest in a simple twitch of the eye or facial muscles. Sometimes, her muscular structure would twitch all at once. Some seizures come and go quietly and quickly. Some linger for minutes and are accompanied by shrieks or screaming noises. The real scary ones obstruct her airways and stop her breathing.

Throughout the years, neurologists tried to control the seizures by daily doses of anti-seizure medications. In addition, she was prescribed Diazepam rectal gel (Diastat Acudial) to be used in case the seizure lasts longer than it should. The Diastat was effective in stopping the seizure most of the time. But it came with a high price. Diastat is a sedating drug. For 48 hours following the use of Diastat, Stephanie would be in a drugged state. Lethargic and sleepy, she could hardly swallow her food which led to food aspiration which in turn led to pneumonia. Being sedated like that made breathing difficult too. Watching her oxygen levels closely became a must. Despite taking her medications religiously, Stephanie continued to have seizures regularly. We were torn about giving her the Diastat and reserved it for the worse seizures. One dosage per seizure was the limit. But a lot of times one dose wasn't enough to stop the seizure. We had to go to the ER for a dose of Ativan.

We definitely were distressed about the seizures, but at the same time we hated the side effects of the drugs. Combining the Diastat and Ativan was not a pleasant experience for her. A few times her lungs collapsed as a side effect of the two drugs combined. I remember one incident very vividly. It was the day after 9/11. We couldn't stop the seizure with Diastat and needed to drive her to NY Presbyterian Hospital. Because of the state of emergency, it was impossible to drive into Manhattan, so we called 911. The ambulance took us to a hospital nearby. Kim and I were terrified because every time she was under the care of a doctor who was unfamiliar with her, bad things happened. Sure enough, they gave her too much sedatives and her lung collapsed. I became frantic. The whole 9/11 situation had everyone on edge. I threatened to sue them if they didn't transfer her to NY Presbyterian immediately. They honored our wish. We stayed in the hospital for a few days until she could breathe on her own again.

For a while after that, Kim and I wanted to take her off the anti-seizure meds. Their side effects were horrible. She was always spaced out and too drugged to respond to her surroundings. Being non-verbal, she could not tell me if she had headaches, felt drowsy or nauseated, all of which are side effects. Besides, they were not effective in controlling the breakthrough of seizures. It wasn't until I had a clash with the head of the PICU that I decided to take action and stop the meds.

At one point, Stephanie was on three different anti-seizure meds. Still, the seizures kept happening. One day she ended up in the PICU for aspirated pneumonia due to the sedating drugs. The staff observed her seizures and suggested we run a 24-hour EEG. When the results came back, the attending doctor requested to see me.

"We would like to add another medicine to Stephanie's protocol. This one is very strong and may cause her to be unaware of her surrounding most of the time," the doctor said.

"Absolutely not," was my reply.

"The EEG showed she has seizure activity in her brain that doesn't manifest outwardly," she argued.

"I'm having a hard time dealing with the seen stuff. I can't worry about the unseen activities too. So again, no new drugs," I insisted.

Stephanie stayed in the hospital for a few days recovering from the pneumonia. During the whole time, I was ambushed by doctors trying to make me agree to their request. They called me at home several times to try and convince me. Fear was creeping into my heart but I knew deep inside that she shouldn't be on any new drugs. As soon as she felt better, I requested her release. I arrived at the PICU that afternoon determined to bring her home with me. The attending doctor had something else planned for me. I was called to the conference room for a meeting. Walking into the room, I felt ambushed and trapped. There sat the PICU's attending doctor, the head nurse practitioner, Stephanie's nurse, the head of the Pediatrics Department of Neurology, and two security guards. I felt like I was on trial.

As if I didn't understand, they proceeded to explain to me how wrong I was in not agreeing with their recommendation. Their argument and attitude came close to accusing me of child neglect. When I refused, the attending doctor slid a paper across the table and asked if I would kindly sign it. I looked at it and shoved it back her way. She was asking me to sign an against medical advice form.

I stood up, ignored everyone else in the room, locked my eyes on her and asked, "Do you have children, Doctor?"

"Yes, two."

"I bet you enjoy every time you come home to their hugs and kisses. You love it when they call your name, don't you?" I asked.

"Very much so. Why do you ask?"

"Unlike most mothers, I care for my daughter day and night not knowing if she even recognizes who I am. I don't get hugs. I don't get kisses. I don't get to hear her say my name. All I get is a rare flicker of light in her eye or a half smile every now and then. Another sedative will take that away completely." I stood there fighting the tears.

They all looked at each other, then at me.

"I am sorry, Faye," the doctor said, "you are free to go."

Kim had Stephanie all packed and ready to leave. I ran out of that room before I exploded. Two days later the doctor called and informed me that the final results of the EEG were inconclusive. Giving her that medication would have been a mistake.

Following that incident, I spoke to her neurologist and set a plan in motion to get her off all anti-seizure meds. It took her 18 months to be completely free. Stephanie still has seizures today. They are not worse than when she was on the medications. We stop them by using acupressure techniques and prayer. We no longer have to worry about lethargy, collapsed lungs, or drug overdose. She is as alert as she can be for her condition.

Respiratory Complications

I've already mentioned Stephanie's struggles with upper respiratory infections and pneumonia. For years this issue caused us a lot of grief. I don't want to repeat myself, but I want to talk about decongestant medications for a brief moment.

Nebulizer treatments are a common practice for treating upper respiratory infections. For a long time, the main drug that was used on her was Albuterol. It was effective, but made her very agitated and spastic. It wasn't until I knew that Albuterol causes children to be hyper that I understood what was going on. Stephanie is bound to a wheelchair and can't run around to burn the extra energy caused by Albuterol. Her system was getting hyper with no outlet to let go of the energy. Naturally, we started requesting the use of other medications. Because she didn't officially have an allergic reaction to Albuterol, we had a difficult time getting the doctors to prescribe alternative medicines. It turns out the hospital will push whichever drug the insurance is willing to pay for. In Stephanie's case, a combination of Xopenex and Pulmicort resulted in the best outcome. However, these were expensive drugs and thus were not preferred by the insurance companies. Kim and I kept on insisting and fighting every time she needed these meds. This is a small example of how we as parents and caregivers must advocate on behalf of our children to ensure they get the best care. Can you guess which medication Stephanie takes when she needs to use a nebulizer? You can bet it's not Albuterol.

Despite all our efforts and the medications she was on, Stephanie had a constant battle with phlegm. Mucus got stuck in her throat and choked her. Chest physiotherapy (CPT) was a necessary part of her daily routine. Any time during the day or night, you could hear Kim pounding on her chest or back to help break up the mucus. Breathing was a labored task for her. Tired of watching her suffer and afraid of the low oxygen levels, we turned to a friend of mine who offered an alternative treatment. Her natural, inexpensive, pain-free and surgery-free method worked like magic. Stephanie has been free from abnormal mucus production for years.

Early Intervention

Stephanie qualified for early intervention services shortly after her diagnosis. Because of her severe disabilities, she required a host of therapeutic services. Soon a bunch of therapists with different specialties flooded our home. From physical and occupational therapists to special education teachers, they all rushed in to offer their expertise in hopes of remedying her condition. It was a race against time. With each passing moment, her brain was growing dimmer. Early on the symptoms weren't as severe and I had hope the therapies would make a difference. But as the months and years passed by my hope slowly faded. So many factors played into that.

First, her brain injury was so severe that her body didn't respond to the stimulations. Second, because of her frequent sicknesses and hospitalizations, her therapy sessions were often disrupted. There was no consistency which is a vital component for a successful therapy outcome. Third, the therapists desired a steady income and did not stick around for a long time. It was difficult for Stephanie to form a bond with her therapists as they changed frequently. In addition to that, I was picky about who got to work with her. I had standards when it came to handling Stephanie. These were rules that made sense to me. I had three simple guidelines: wash your hands before each session, do not smell like a chimney, and do not show up if you are sick or you've been around a sick child. You can't imagine how many therapists thought I was asking the impossible of them.

Soon after Stephanie turned four, the social worker talked to me about sending her to school the following year. Early intervention services stopped at age five and we lived near one of the top schools for special needs children in NYC. They invited me to check out the facility before I enrolled her. The school was clean and it had various programs for the children. She would have had all her therapy during the school day. I toured the different rooms and was shown all the equipment meant to assist the children in their development. Walking into her future classroom I saw the other children in their wheelchairs. I could not imagine my daughter in this place. I'm not belittling the efforts or the intentions of the staff. But two women are not enough to take care of a classroom of physically-challenged children. I grabbed a tissue and started to wipe the drool from their faces. I thought about Stephanie waiting her turn to be fed or for her diaper to be changed and I made my decision to homeschool her.

I don't know if that was the best decision as far as her education, but I know I did my best to provide her with everything she needed. I took her education very seriously. I didn't spare any money, time, nor energy in looking for answers for her condition. I enrolled her with The National Association of Child Development. They evaluated her and provided us with a neurodevelopment home program that we followed daily. It was tedious work, but we didn't complain. We saw some small improvements. Then we tried the methods recommended by the Family Hope Center, another child development specialist. We followed their protocol for a few years. Again, the results were minute.

I already mentioned previously all our attempts to make her life easier. We never lost hope in God's willingness or ability to heal her. We just wanted to do everything in our power to help her too. However, the severity of her brain injury was too much for us to conquer. All the supplements and therapies gave only temporary relief. Nothing offered lasting and permanent change. The only steady thing that always gave us hope was prayer. Every time we got stuck in a tough spot, we cried out to God and He delivered us.

CHAPTER TEN
Family Dynamics

So far, I have been sharing with you the events surrounding our daughter Stephanie over the past eighteen years. I would now like to go deeper and share how this impacted our family in the day-to-day affairs.

Stephanie altered our lives in more than one way. I don't know how things would have looked if she had been any different. All I know is she altered the course of our family and was the influential trigger for many decisions. Having a special needs child complicates more than just daily routines, caring for such a child also exposes you to many unusual experiences. You are faced with difficult decisions. Sometimes it even forces you to walk down some unpleasant paths. A special needs child also expands your horizon in many areas and if you allow it, they will enlarge your heart and increase your capacity to fully embrace life.

As Ted and I dealt with the initial trauma of losing Deborah and the uncertainty of Stephanie's survival, we realized we were entering a new emotional territory that might produce unwanted results if we were not careful. We valued our relationship and desired to protect it to the best of our ability. The divorce rate is higher in couples dealing with a special needs child than the general population. Even though Ted and I never entertained the idea, we felt the strain Stephanie's illness placed on our relationship. I'm so grateful to say that this year we celebrated our twenty-fifth wedding anniversary. Our marriage not only survived, but it thrived. We actually grew stronger and more intimate through it all.

The first thing we did was to acknowledge the situation. We did not ignore the traumatic event. We realized what was going on, and that it would take a toll on our emotional and mental state.

Extending Grace

In the first few years, when we lived in emergency mode, we agreed we would put the majority of our efforts into sustaining the older children and stabilizing Stephanie's situation. Our main objective was to care for the children and on most days, we did not have the emotional capacity to care for each other. During that season, we withdrew from our love account instead of depositing in it. This meant that we both operated with grace and forgiveness toward each other. We extended patience and kindness when shortcomings and bad tempers surfaced. Our love account was full and allowed us to withdraw from it until life somewhat stabilized. We had intentionally invested in our love account for years prior to Stephanie's incident. That gave us a secure foundation to stand upon. It is vital for couples to deposit and invest in their relationship on a daily basis.

Another wise move we took was to communicate honestly. We did not wear masks or pretend to feel or be anything that was not truthful. We communicated our frustration, anger, fear, or despair without judging each other. We also communicated and agreed about our roles. We worked as a team. Understanding our roles minimized friction and kept our expectations of each other clear and realistic. When it came to Stephanie's care, I assumed the leading role which included making decisions regarding therapy, medications, or procedures. I also was the primary caregiver for the first year of her life. Ted was an amazing supporter. He took the night shifts during her frequent hospital stays. The nurses called him "Silly Noises Dad" because he made silly sounds to entertain Stephanie. The staff told us that they knew when Stephanie was on the floor because they could hear Ted's singing. He also cared for the older two children when I wasn't home. He prayed for and with me. With his wisdom and solid insight, he helped me make the difficult decisions. But above all, his devotion, commitment, and stability were my anchor during the many storms.

Even though Stephanie's condition dominated our lives and took the majority of our energy and time, we were careful to keep some activities consistent for the sake of the children and our own sanity. Going to church every Sunday was sacred. We needed to be in God's presence and in fellowship with the body of Christ. We made sure the children didn't miss school unless it was absolutely unavoidable. The routine helped to keep the anxiety down. Ted and I even sneaked a date night here and there so we could recharge.

We were totally honest and transparent with the children from day one. We didn't hide things from them. We explained everything that was happening in age appropriate language. We encouraged them to express their emotions without judgment. We welcomed their questions and had them accompany us to the hospital as much as possible. We allowed them to see us as we struggled to manage the situation. We shared our hopes, fears, doubts and faith with them. They saw us rejoice in the small victories and they witnessed us cry in frustration. Above all, they saw us hold on to God in every situation, love them without ceasing and support each other daily.

Homeschool

One major way Stephanie affected our family was the decision to homeschool our children. This was not something I had contemplated beforehand. I wasn't even aware of such a method of education. During the first two years of Stephanie's life, her health emergencies were frequent and intense. I practically lived in the hospital. Upon graduating from second grade, my oldest daughter, Rebecca, was presented with an award for achieving the highest score on a test given to her age group in NYC. I was very proud, of course, and terrified at the same time. As I sat at the award ceremony, I thought about the school year. All of a sudden, I realized how uninvolved I was in her education. For the entirety of second grade, I hardly remembered helping with homework or knowing what went on in school. The year went by like a blur. I was not okay with that.

I knew in my heart Stephanie's condition was not a short-term project and sacrifices must be made. But I was not willing to sacrifice the other two children or my relationship with them. So, I prayed. I asked God to give me a way to be able to attend to and connect with all three children at the time. Soon enough the idea of homeschooling came to me. I researched it and decided to give it a try. The plan was to do it for one year only. I just wanted to reconnect with Rebecca and Theodore and to make sure they were not lost in the middle of the chaos.

> I ASKED GOD TO GIVE ME A WAY TO BE ABLE TO ATTEND TO AND CONNECT WITH ALL THREE CHILDREN AT THE SAME TIME

This year marks our sixteenth and last year of homeschooling. It has been an eventful journey to say the least. All my children were homeschooled. Rebecca graduated high school from home at age sixteen. She started college before she turned seventeen. Theodore transferred to a private high school in ninth grade and graduated from there. Daniel, my youngest, is currently in the same high school that Theodore attended. Even Stephanie was homeschooled. We did all her therapy and education at home.

Hiring a Nanny

Hiring a nanny was another major change in our lifestyle. This was not an easy decision for me. The first ten months of Stephanie's life were brutal and took a toll on my body and my soul. I was handed from one emergency to another like a hot potato. Illnesses, seizures, fevers and hospital visits were happening at a faster rate than I could handle. I had no time to breathe or make sense of what was going on. For months, Ted tried to convince me to hire a live-in nanny to help me care for Stephanie or to give me a break. I kept refusing the idea. I couldn't hand over my role as the primary caregiver to anyone else. I couldn't imagine someone else would be able to love and care for her the way I did. Stephanie could not speak and she depended on me to be her advocate. We had developed a special, strong bond of communication. How could I betray her by letting another person in?

However, Ted saw how worn down I'd become toward the end of the first year. He recognized the unmet needs of the older two children. He insisted on hiring a nanny. He already had someone in mind we both had known for years, which made the decision a bit more bearable. Kim moved in with us in the summer of 2000 and she's been taking care of Stephanie ever since. Gradually, she took over her care. She has been such a blessing to us. I never thought a woman could love a child as much as Kim loves Stephanie. She tirelessly watches over her day and night and attends to all her needs. Through thick and thin, ups and downs, Kim has been a faithful companion. She not only took care of Stephanie, but she also helped with the other children. She supported and encouraged me as I continued my education. Without her I wouldn't be able to do what I do today. I'm forever in her debt. I have the deepest gratitude and regard for her in my heart.

Saying all this doesn't mean we always had a smooth ride. Family dynamics change when you adopt another person into your household. Soon enough both parties must adjust their behaviors and expectations in order to live in peace with each other. Sometimes boundaries become blurry and we step on each other's toes. Unspoken or unclear expectations create unpleasant situations that are dangerous to navigate sometimes. Even though we had a satisfying and deep friendship in general, we also challenged each other in ways that were uncomfortable to say the least. But all in all, we learned how to forgive each other, pray for one another and lean on each other to go through life. And when push came to shove we knew Stephanie depended on both of us to make it through. We became a team with one purpose in mind: help Stephanie become the person God created her to be.

Truth be told, Stephanie altered the direction of our life as a family and as individuals. Some things were for the best and others were not. The children were exposed to pain, sickness, death, frustration, and brokenness at an early age. They had to learn how to respond to emergencies like seizures and helping to replace a malfunctioning feeding tube. They probably know more about medical terminology than the average person. I know they have more compassion and tolerance towards people with special needs because of their sister. But they also had to deal with anxiety and fear. They had to make peace with canceled vacations and an absent mom on occasions. All of us grew and matured significantly because of Stephanie which is a desired outcome of a tragedy. However, we all paid a price.

Families who care for someone with special needs must navigate all the usual family dysfunctions, but with the added strain of someone who is totally dependent on their care and unable to contribute in the usual ways we recognize reciprocity. It is a difficult world, and few understand what it is really like to love and live in this kind of long-lasting, extreme situation. Many families fall apart under the strain. I am blessed beyond measure that ours has learned how to thrive and flourish.

I desire to encourage you to nurture yourself and your family, no matter how difficult the challenges you face. Whatever your family dynamics may be, ask God to show you how to strengthen the bonds of love that hold you together.

CHAPTER ELEVEN
Daniel's Story

Ted loves children. He always wanted to have as many as possible. By the time Stephanie was two years old, he was yearning for another baby. I couldn't understand it. Wasn't he scared to have another traumatic experience? What if we had another physically challenged child? It wasn't that I was against the idea of having a baby. After all, we had never really gotten the chance to enjoy the last experience. But I was terrified of the thought of having another sick child. I avoided coming near Ted anytime I might've had the chance to conceive. Even though I longed for a baby, I allowed fear to prevent me from moving forward.

The spring of 2002 we were busy settling into our new home. I remember that day vividly. It was Memorial Day weekend. We'd just received a truckload of soil for our front yard. All day on Saturday I was busy shoveling dirt and working in the garden. I felt weak and nauseated towards evening time. Getting suspicious, I asked Ted to buy me a pregnancy test. You can imagine my surprise when the test showed positive for pregnancy. Just to make sure, I sent Ted back to the pharmacy to purchase another test. He was dancing around the house when the second test confirmed the same result. For a moment, I felt joy and relief. Joy because I was happy to carry another life. Relief because God didn't leave it up to me to decide when to get pregnant. I knew if

He had left it up to me, I would have not been brave enough to do it. I would have missed the chance to meet the most amazing Daniel in the whole world.

Getting rid of the fear was neither easy nor a swift task. I actually struggled with it for months, starting from the second day I found out I was pregnant until about two months before I gave birth. I made an appointment to see my OB/GYN doctor right after Memorial Day. His reaction to my news was not comforting. After confirming the pregnancy for himself, he called me to his office.

"You can't get pregnant now, not after what you went through in your last pregnancy," he started. "What were you thinking? Your uterus can't carry a baby to a full term. We had to cut it vertically during the last emergency C-section. The cervix is too weak to stay sealed for the whole pregnancy."

He looked at me intensely. His countenance betraying his feelings.

My heart was sinking further and further in my chest with every word he uttered.

I fought back my tears and asked, "What am I to do?"

With concern written on his face, he told me I was taking a big risk by carrying this baby.

"The best scenario," he continued, "would be having a miscarriage within a few weeks. The worst scenario is going into early labor again and repeating the same experience as last time. In any case I don't see a bright outcome for you." He paused for a moment.

The very air was heavy between us. "There is always ..." he looked down for a moment, then finished, "... there is always the option to abort, of course."

I looked at him and shook my head no. "Abortion is not an option for me." I said with great feeling. "I am already in love with this child. God gave him to me and I will trust that everything will be just fine. God will give me the grace to make it if I end up with another special baby."

This declaration basically concluded our conversation. He asked the nurse to transfer my case to a high-risk specialist at the hospital. They made me an appointment in two weeks to go see the new doctor.

Nothing out of the ordinary happened in the next two weeks. I kept my pregnancy news a secret from the rest of the family. Only Ted, Kim, and my parents knew. I didn't want to disappoint the children in case anything bad happened. On the day of the appointment I drove to the hospital to see the high-risk specialist. This particular doctor oversaw women with complicated pregnancies, including women who had a hard time conceiving. The staff took a brief medical history, but they could not perform the necessary tests that day. I returned the next day ready for a transvaginal ultrasound. The doctor checked me for a brief moment, asked me to get dressed and left the room. A few moments later he entered the room accompanied with his assistant.

"How did you get here?" he asked.

I answered that I had driven myself. Upon learning this, he asked if I could have someone pick me up.

"Why, What's wrong?" I panicked.

"The amniotic sac is already protruding out of the uterus. You should be laying down as much as possible until we perform a cervical cerclage. My next available date is next week. It is possible you could have a miscarriage before then."

I just looked at him stunned and speechless. I called my brother to come pick me up and sat down to fill out the necessary paperwork for the procedure.

The time between my appointment and the procedure went by very slowly. I battled doubt and fear every moment. I laid in bed trying to stay still. I had a mini heart attack every time I had to pee. I checked and rechecked the toilet before I flushed in case the baby dropped down. It was torture. I wondered how I was going to handle seven more months of this. Finally, the day arrived and the doctor was able to perform the procedure. He gently pushed the baby sac back into the uterus. He then partially sewed the cervix, 28 mm out of 40 mm. He placed me on medications to prevent labor contractions and ordered strict bed rest until my delivery time.

I was thankful the procedure was successful even if not 100%. I was willing to do whatever it took to keep my baby safe. I adhered to the doctor's instructions very closely. I even homeschooled my two children from bed. I was allowed to shower once a week, the day I went in for my checkup. Otherwise, I spent 98% of my day laying on my back. The anti-contraction medicine had unpleasant side effects. It lowered my already low blood pressure. To counter this I added more salt to my diet than I usually allow myself. The added sodium plus the sedentary life style caused me to retain fluids and gain a lot of weight. I was at risk of developing thrombosis in my lower extremities. My mother took special care to massage my legs and back often to bring relief to my sore and aching muscles and to assist in circulating the blood. Twice my blood pressure plummeted and I fainted. During one of those episodes, I even had a seizure. None of this deterred me. I was willing to go to any measure to have this baby.

> I WAS WILLING TO DO WHATEVER IT TOOK TO KEEP MY BABY SAFE

What's In a Name?

Choosing a name for the baby was a bit of a challenge. Once we knew it was a boy, Ted and I began to think of different names to call him. He got to name our first born and one of the twins, while I chose the name for our second child and the other twin. It wasn't a competition, but we both wanted to name this baby. I had my heart set on Samuel or Daniel, both biblical characters dear to my heart. Ted didn't want to name him Samuel because we already had a Samuel in our immediate family. He wasn't sure about Daniel either.

For days, he kept saying, "I love this baby so much, I will just call him Beloved."

What sort of name is that? I thought to myself until one morning an idea came to my mind.

"Ted," I said to him as he got ready to go to work, "Who in the Bible was nicknamed Beloved?"

He looked at me, sighed, threw his hands up in the air and said nothing. It was settled. We would call him Daniel (Daniel 10:19).

Battling Fear

Throughout the pregnancy I wrestled with fear and uncertainty. Even though friends were praying and speaking into my baby's life, I still was afraid that something bad would happen. My doctor, who I saw once a week, was continuously reminding me of all the reasonable and unfavorable outcomes of the pregnancy. In my seventh month, he noted his concern about the baby's weight. He would give it 2-3 weeks and if the baby didn't gain enough weight, I would have to give myself daily steroid shots. The idea of giving myself shots terrified me. This added to my fear and multiplied my doubts. I became nervous and upset to the point I couldn't sleep at night.

One day I got in the shower and I started violently crying and yelling to God. I needed peace. I needed Him to say something to comfort me. When I stepped out of the shower, I grabbed my Bible, threw it open with my eyes closed and placed my finger on a verse.

"Please speak to me," I cried out to God.

I had never done that before ... or since. I looked down at this verse:

> "No one shall suffer miscarriage or be barren in your land; I will fulfill the number of your days."
> Exodus 23:26

At that moment I received that verse as if God was telling me I would not lose the baby and everything would be fine. I thanked Him. As soon as I surrendered to Him, His peace washed over me and stayed with me until the day I delivered Daniel.

That same day I went for my checkup. The doctor poked around with his camera as usual, took measurements of the baby, and was satisfied with his growth and weight. However, he wasn't ready for what he saw next. He kept moving the camera from one angle to another and checked his findings again and again. He then called his nurse practitioner and asked her to double check his conclusions. When she confirmed his suspicion, he looked at me with a puzzled look.

"I would not have believed it if I heard it from anyone else. But since I did the surgery myself, I would have to agree that we just witnessed a miracle! Your cervix is completely shut."

This doctor did not particularly believe God existed, but at that moment I felt brave enough to share my encounter with him. His facial expression changed from surprise to admiration.

"Please make a copy of that verse for me. I will include it in your file. When I teach about your case, I will mention to my students that your faith helped save your child."

He smiled at me and I smiled back.

Peace to Plan

I was at peace from that day on. Check-ins became much more relaxing and pleasant. Ted and I started to plan for the nursery and were counting the days until Daniel's arrival. As I approached my due date, I became heavier and heavier. Sleep became an illusion. I basically spent seven months within the walls of my room. Stephanie came to visit me occasionally. She would lay in bed with me and watch me teach her siblings. On the brighter side, in the final 6-8 weeks of pregnancy, I was allowed to sit in a recliner chair. Ted bought me a nice one which my children dubbed "the queen's throne." Ted kept our date night tradition. Once a week, he would order in and we ate in bed, talked, or watched a movie together.

> WHEN I TEACH ABOUT YOUR CASE, I WILL MENTION TO MY STUDENTS THAT YOUR FAITH HELPED SAVE YOUR CHILD

Because of the cerclage procedure I had earlier in my pregnancy, it was dangerous for me to carry the baby to full term (40 weeks). Having labor contractions was too risky. The uterus might rip and I would bleed internally which would put both my life and the baby's life at risk. For this reason, the doctor chose January 23 as the day to have a scheduled c-section. He concluded this date was far enough from my actual due date that I wouldn't have any natural contractions, but safe enough for the baby to be born healthy. Even though I understood the science behind this protocol, I didn't like the idea of a scheduled c-section. I'd already given up the notion of a natural birth, but I didn't want the doctor to choose the day my baby was born. I wished for Daniel to come out when he was ready. There was one person that could solve this dilemma, Father God. Once again, I found myself on my knees (figuratively), asking him for Daniel's safe arrival.

Send Me a Sign

In simple child-like faith, I asked Father God an unusual request. I prayed He would give me a sign before the contractions began so I could get to the hospital on time. I imagined in my mind what the sign would be. Only Ted knew about this request. Every day and night I waited patiently for the sign. I knew in my heart that Father God would answer me. Sure enough, at 3:00 am on January 21, two days before the appointed c-section, the sign showed up. It was exactly the way I imagined it in my mind. I excitedly woke Ted and motioned for him to get out of bed. He figured it was time to go. We grabbed our hospital bag and headed out. It was almost 6:00 a.m. when we arrived at the hospital. As soon as the sliding doors opened, my contractions started strong and steady.

I was immediately rushed into the operating room. My previous deal with the doctor was to be given full anesthesia. I just wanted to go to sleep and wake up when it was over. However, the doctor changed his mind while I was wheeled into the OR and announced I was getting an epidural shot instead. That was not the best decision. It took the anesthesiologist eight tries to find the right spot in my spine. Meanwhile, I had to curve my back in C shape for him, hold my breath and stay still while he stuck his long needle between my vertebra in and out eight times. All this while having serious contractions.

Finally, the drugs took effect and my lower body went numb. Within a few seconds I developed a reaction to the drug. My upper body, including my head, started to shake violently and uncontrollably. The doctor could not perform the surgery as I almost slipped off the table. The OR team attached arm extensions to the table, spread my arms like a T and strapped them down. The nurse also strapped my head and chest to the table. Ted leaned over my chest to help keep me still. Thankfully, this episode ended as soon as the doctor obtained Daniel out of the uterus.

Strong and vibrant, his cries filled the room like a joyful song. I saw his perfect face through sheets of tears, smiled, and whispered a prayer of thanksgiving to my Father God.

STRONG AND VIBRANT, HIS
CRIES FILLED THE ROOM
LIKE A JOYFUL SONG

CHAPTER TWELVE
Still Waiting

This story is about our family's journey with Stephanie, but it's also about my transformation into the woman I am today. It all began with a simple prayer: "My heart longs to know You more. I lay down all that I am to encounter you at a deeper level." This was my heart's desire for three years leading up to the events of August 1999. I don't see God as the source of the tragedy, but I do know He took advantage of the tragedy to shape me into who I am at this moment. And for that, I am eternally grateful.

Writing this book was not an easy task for me. My purpose was to offer an authentic account of our family's journey. That mandated vulnerability and transparency. I also desired to encourage others who are going through similar trails. That called for humility as I exposed my weaknesses and failures. In addition, going through the details of all the events forced me to pause, remember, and think about the actions and the decisions that were taken then. I stopped and reevaluated my decisions and wondered if I had made the right choices or not. With each memory came a flood of emotions. Some brought healing and closure while others brought regret and more questions begging to be answered. I treaded very carefully as I allowed the memories to surface. I needed to channel the right amount of emotions to make the story authentic, but not allow them too much free reign or they would overwhelm me and throw me into a pit of despair.

With the flood of memories also surfaced many wounds. I relied fully on the Holy Spirit to distinguish between the ones I was healed from and the ones I needed to address. Sometimes when we're emotionally overwhelmed the enemy tries to use old wounds that were already dealt with to make us doubt the healing and open the door for defeat all over again. I wish I could tell you I was always successful in balancing my emotions. I was not. But I can tell you one thing for sure: writing this book pushed me even further into my Father's arms and I relied on His grace to carry me through. Day by day I experienced His relentless love and goodness.

I started out writing this book with confidence, hoping to give satisfying answers to my questions about life's trials and pain. But as I unpacked my heart and allowed myself to be transparent with God and others, I found out I had more questions than answers. I got discouraged at one point and contemplated terminating the whole project. But then I came to realize I don't have to have all the answers to be happy. I rest assured on the solid truth that God is good to all. He has it all figured out and I trust Him. Our adventure continues as we seek Him and He guides us through life's mountains and valleys. Struggles make our victories much more valuable. Rainy days wash away the dirt and make us long for and enjoy the sun even more.

Holding On

Do not let your pain and suffering drag you down. Hold on to your faith. Persevere and be patient. Rejoice in today's trials for they will make you stronger. Above all be thankful in the good times and in the not so good times. Always know He is beside you and with you. His love never fails. You are not alone. You are a part of a glorious body. You are a valuable member in a community of warriors. You have a role to play in shaping the history of the Kingdom. His grace abounds in you. His mercy and goodness chase after you all the days of your life. The best is yet to come.

I still hold on to His promise to heal Stephanie. I don't know why it hasn't happened yet, but I know it will. As I wrote, I dreamed about completing the last chapter just in time for her to wake up from her long battle and find her brain miraculously healed of all damage. My hopes built as I wrote. I grew expectant, then when it didn't happen I felt that familiar let-down, not quite yet ...

How can I write a story that isn't finished? I asked myself. Even figuring out the title proved a significant challenge. I wanted to share authentically from my journey as well as be clear that my belief Stephanie will be completely whole is unwavering. I am not delusional. I am not in denial.

Be assured, not only do I believe God is able to heal my Stephanie, but I also believe He desires to heal her. I believe in living heaven on earth. I do not pursue God for what He will do for me. I chase after Him because He is the origin of my life, the love of my heart, the one who occupies my mind—my perfect Father. Bottom line, whether I see Stephanie healed on this side of heaven or not, He will always have my heart, my devotion, and my life. It is well with my soul.

Declaring My Faith

When I first felt the nudge in my heart to write a chapter about Stephanie's healing before it actually happened, I was puzzled. I tried to ignore it for a over two months, but it kept coming back. I felt it strongly in my heart to write about her healing—even though she was still confined to her wheelchair. After I surrendered to the whisper and agreed to write the chapter, the question was, "Okay, what do I write?" I attempted several approaches and contemplated a couple of ideas, but nothing seemed to work out. The words were stuck and I was confused.

One Sunday morning the Holy Spirit spoke to me during church service and I knew exactly what to write. "Declare your faith regarding her healing," He told me. So, this chapter is a declaration of faith and a prophetic proclamation. Please remember that as of this writing my daughter is still a prisoner of her disability.

I believe that by faith I can create a different reality. I can call on things that are in God's heart for Stephanie. My faith can make her healing a physical reality. God came to Abraham and told him that his descendants would be as numerous as the stars. Meanwhile, Abraham could not have children and had passed the natural age for conceiving. Nonetheless, by faith, he was able to see his descendants and trusted in God's word. Abraham was considered a righteous man because of his faith. On several occasions the Lord spoke to me in dreams, visions, or through other believers about Stephanie's healing.

I trust in Your word, Lord. I choose to believe that Stephanie is walking, talking, and living a normal life. When I look at her sitting helplessly in her wheelchair, I see beyond the disability. I see her playing the piano and traveling around the world telling her story. I see her swimming in the ocean, I hear her sing. Oh, what a beautiful voice she has!

> WHEN I LOOK AT HER SITTING HELPLESSLY IN HER WHEELCHAIR, I SEE BEYOND THE DISABILITY

By faith Sarah was able to conceive even though her womb was dead. Life came from a dead object. The same way I have faith that life will flow from all the dead cells in Stephanie's brain. I declare healing to the neurotransmitters. I see the nerves connecting and flowing between the brain and every cell in her body. Jesus stood outside Lazarus' grave and called his name. Life returned to Lazarus' body and he walked out of the grave. In the name of Jesus, I call out to Stephanie's brain, "Come forth. Come back to life." Jairus had faith that Jesus could bring his daughter from the dead. And Jesus did! He took her hand and pulled her back from the clutches of death. The same thing happened to the widow's son. He was called back to life as he laid in his coffin. Death has no power against Jesus' authority. Death tried to keep Him in the ground but it didn't succeed because the power of resurrection resides in Jesus. A partially dead brain is not a major task for Him to heal. I believe that He is able and willing.

Jesus taught us to pray "on earth as it is in heaven." So I pray "in Stephanie's body as it is in heaven." Sickness and disease do not exist in heaven. Therefore, sickness and disease have no right or authority to reside in her body. There's no pain and suffering in heaven. I believe that it is God's perfect will for her to be free from pain. There's no malfunctioning body parts in heaven. I boldly command all brain damage and disease to depart from Stephanie's body in the name of Jesus.

Everything that Jesus came to accomplish here on earth and everything He demonstrated and spoke about proves to me that healing is my right and inheritance. I'm not going to let anything nor anyone cheat my daughter of this right. "It is finished," Jesus cried on the cross. Done! Everything was paid for and that included lifting off the curse of sickness. No longer does sin, condemnation, fear, or sickness have any authority on us. He fulfilled Isaiah's words: "... but He was pierced for our transgressions, He was crushed for our iniquities; the punishment that brought us peace was on Him, and by his wounds we are healed." I declare that Stephanie is healed because of what Jesus did on the cross. Stephanie is redeemed by the blood of Jesus. Redemption is a full package that includes physical, emotional, and spiritual healing—forgiveness of sin and deliverance.

The Bible says that Jesus went around doing good and healing people. He had compassion for people and his heart broke over their suffering. I believe that Jesus is so good and full of love, mercy, and compassion that

He heals my daughter because He doesn't want her to suffer. I trust in His heart's intentions towards my daughter. I trust in His timing, I trust in His compassion and goodness.

My Prayer

Father, It's not about me or how big my faith is. It's all about You and Your glory. I can feel the joy in my heart and the excitement over her healing. Oh, Father, the day she gets up ... what a glorious day that will be! That will be a God-kind-of-day. You are the God of impossible things. You made a way for Your people by drying up the sea. You make a way for Stephanie to get out of her chair. You challenged nature on several occasions and won each time. You stopped the sun in its place. You calmed the storm. You even changed the molecules of water and turned them into wine. Command Stephanie's brain to function and exchange the dead cells with live ones.

Nothing and no disease stands in Your way. Your garment dried up the woman's bleeding. I stretch my hand right now by faith and touch your garment. Leprosy could not stay in your presence. Distance doesn't hinder You. The centurion asked You to say a word. One word from You healed his son. You are the word that was sent from heaven to heal us. Say a word and Stephanie will be healed. Jesus I have faith in You. I trust in You. You are good. You are faithful. No matter the root cause of the sickness, You are powerful enough to heal. No demon can stand in Your way. Brain damage, no matter how severe, cannot stand in Your way. In the same way the four friends dropped the paralyzed man before You, I lay Stephanie at Your feet. I will keep bringing her to You until she is made whole. I believe in a different reality—a reality where I see her running around, jumping, and driving a car. I dare to see her having a family of her own. I will never accept the wheelchair as her destiny. Not with Jesus as my God.

Jesus, You have power over blindness. You gave sight back. You are correcting her vision even now. You are healing the connection between her eyes and her brain. You made the mute speak. You are healing her vocal chords at this moment. I can hear her voice filling the air with the sound of praise.

Above all, I love You, Father. I am thankful for Stephanie. I am thankful for all the trials, pain, and suffering. Thank You for all the miracles you performed along the way. Thank You for Your grace that carried us through the years. Thank You for the people You sent our way to help, to encourage, and to guide us. Thank You for Stephanie's life and all the wonderful things You have done in her and through her. Thank You for all the lessons that we learned because of her. Thank You for all the awesome plans You have for her and us. I trust that all things will work out for our good and Your glory. In Jesus' name, amen.

While Healing Comes

And now I continue to wait with patient, hopeful expectation. I continue to nurture and care for Stephanie and pour love on her and on Ted and on our other children. I continue to grow and develop and lead a full and wonderful life, embracing every blessing, walking through every challenge, and believing God is good every single day. All of this I freely give myself to while healing comes ...

PHOTO GALLERY
Stephanie in Pictures

Merry Christmas!

Happy Easter!

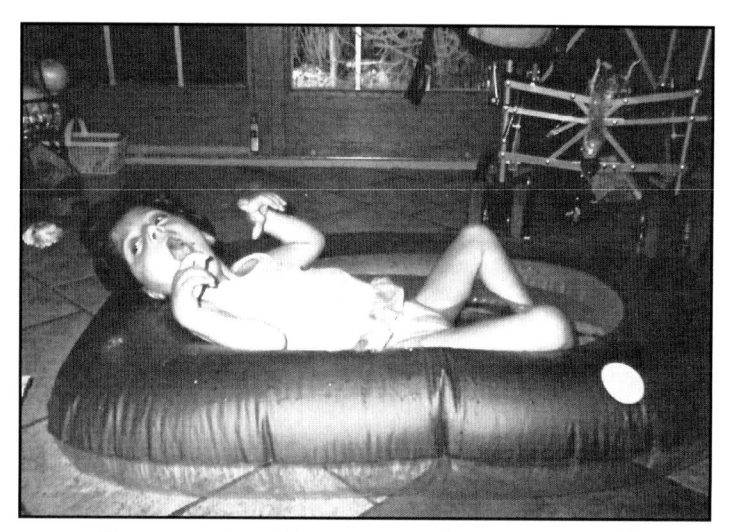

It's too hot outside ... my raft is now a pool!

My last photo before surgery on my teeth

PHOTO GALLERY | 97

A happy day at Sesame Place with Elmo

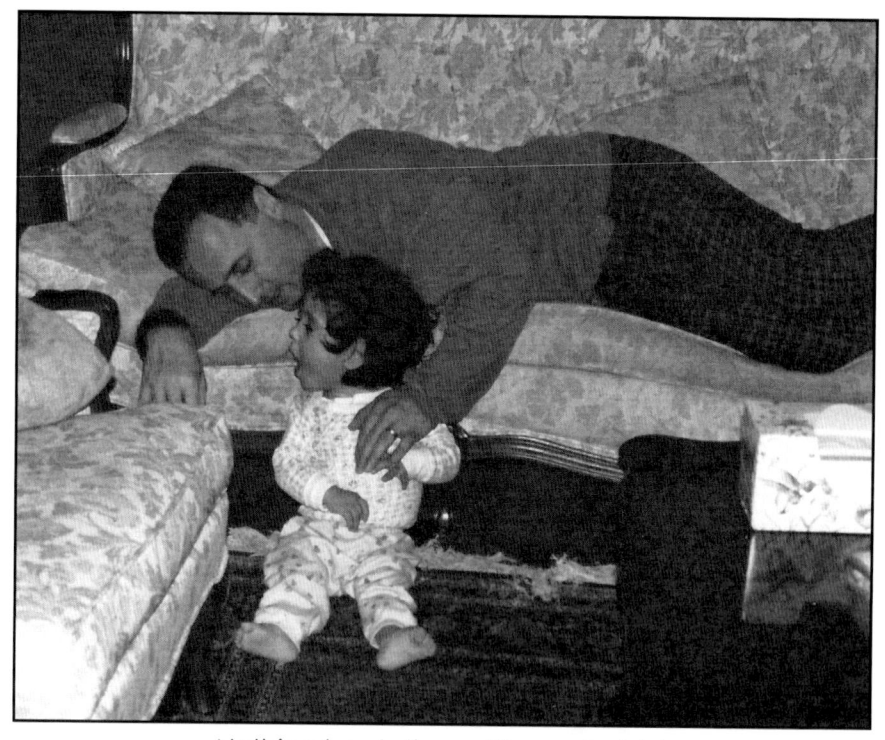

Nothing beats time with my daddy!

Christmas with my family

PHOTO GALLERY | 99

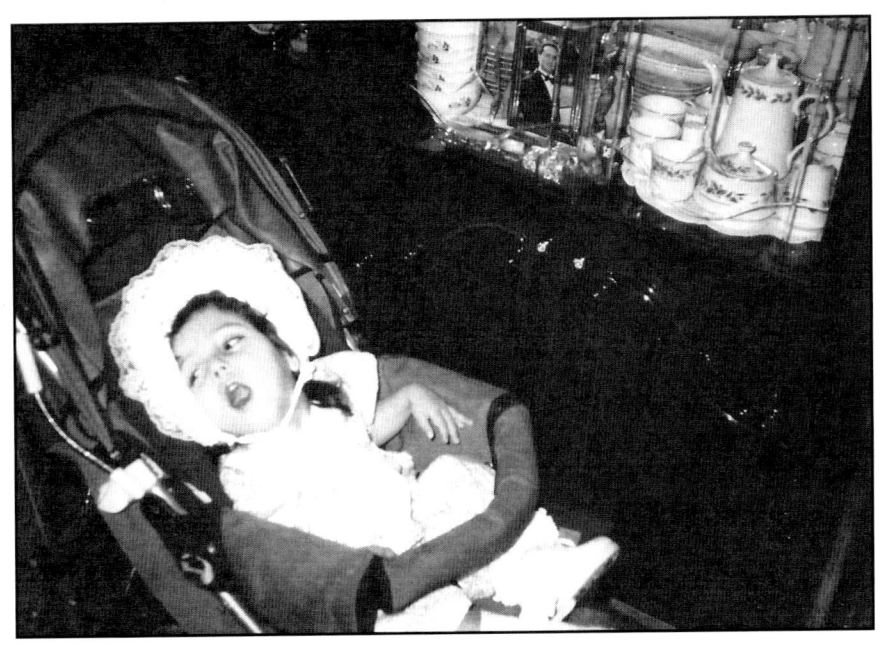

Just chillin' in my stroller

With my whole family

Dad likes to play too

PHOTO GALLERY | 101

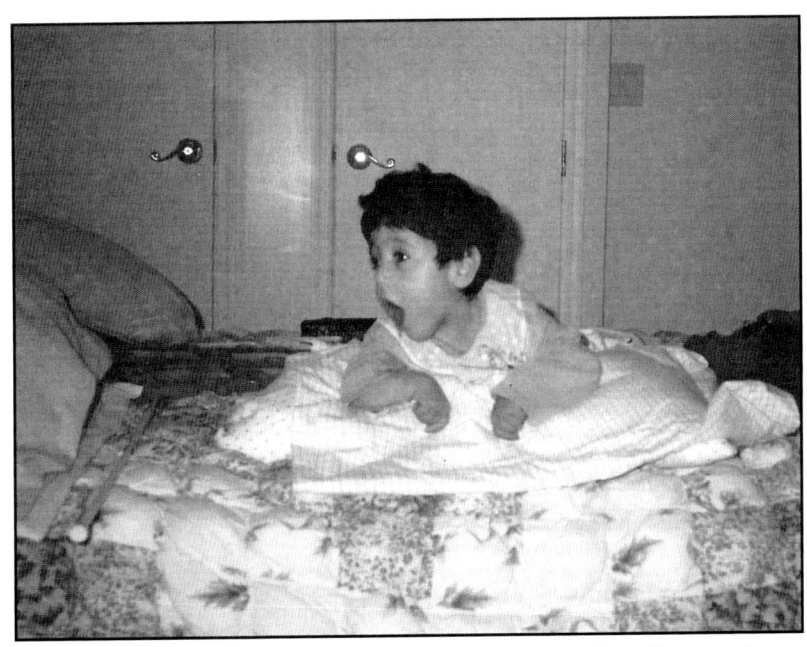

Look at me! I am showing off my progress after therapy!

I feel safest in my daddy's arms

102 | WHILE HEALING COMES

Time to pick apples

I wonder what it is like to ride a bicycle?

PHOTO GALLERY | 103

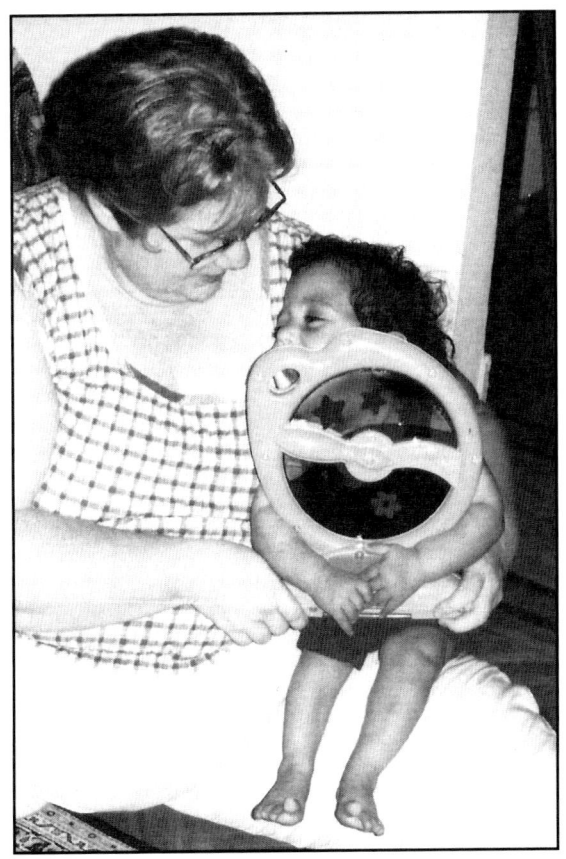

Kim knows my favorite toy

I love my high chair, even when I can't lift my head

104 | WHILE HEALING COMES

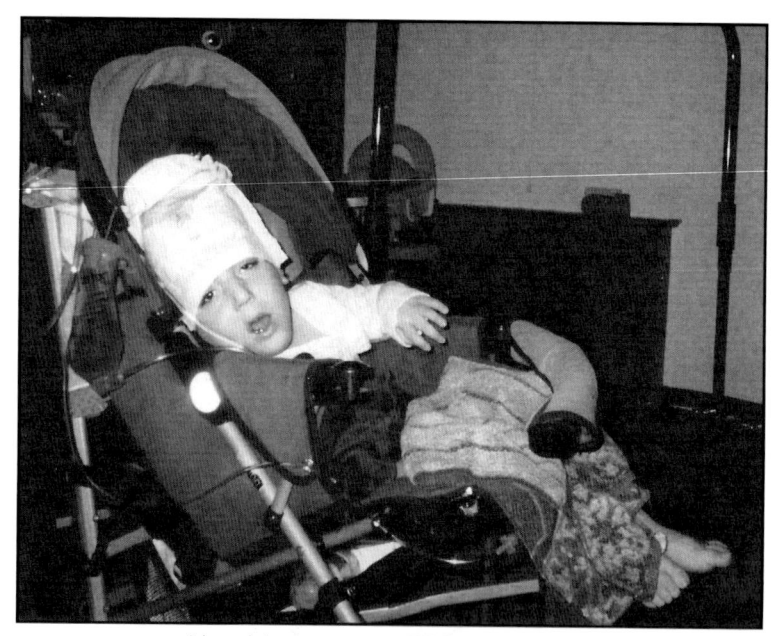

I had to have an EEG at home

At the riding academy with Kim and Theodore

PHOTO GALLERY | 105

Snow Day! ... Hangin' out with Theodore and Rebecca is fun!

I wonder what is in this package? I LOVE Christmas!

This is my favorite doll ...

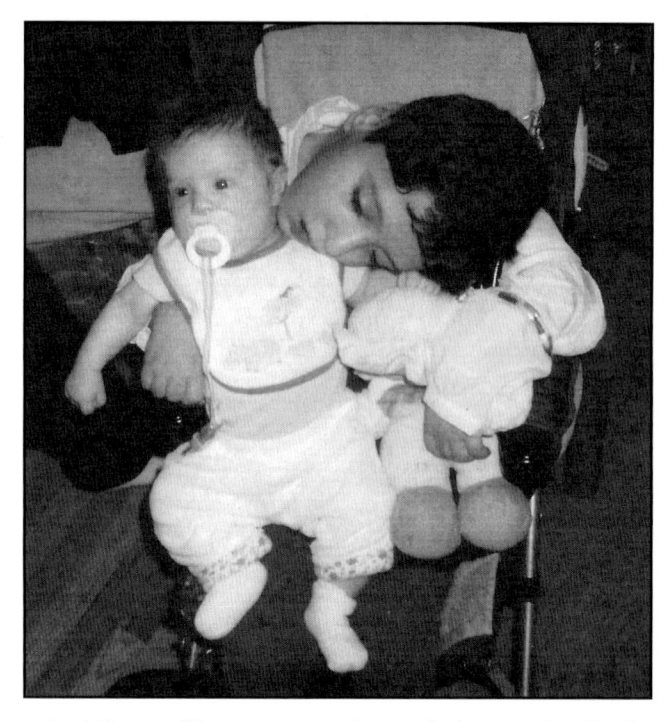

... but time with my second cousin is even better!

PHOTO GALLERY | 107

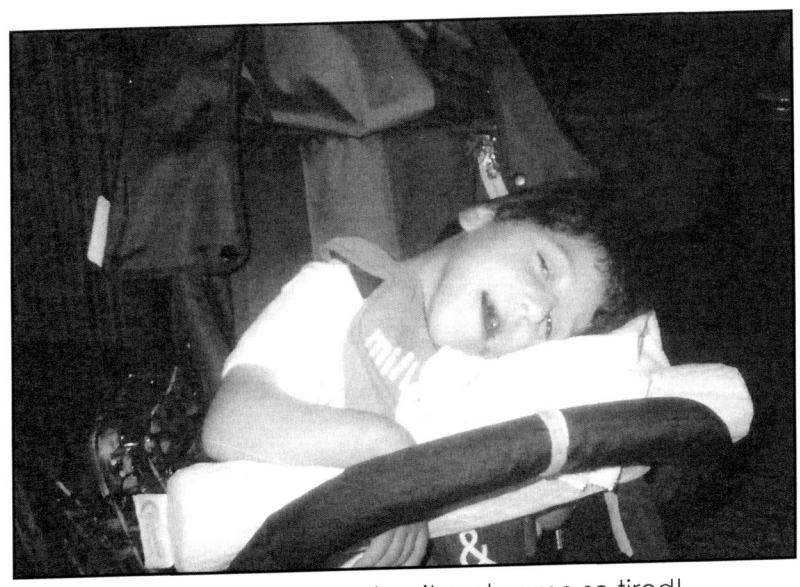

Therapy is hard work ... it makes me so tired!

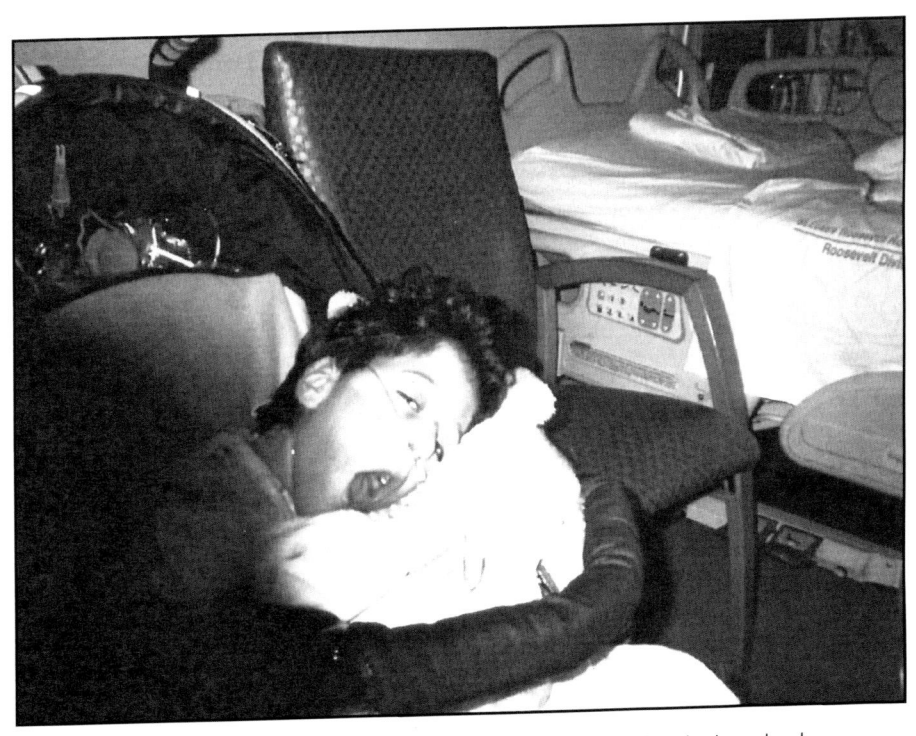

In the hospital again because my airway is obstructed

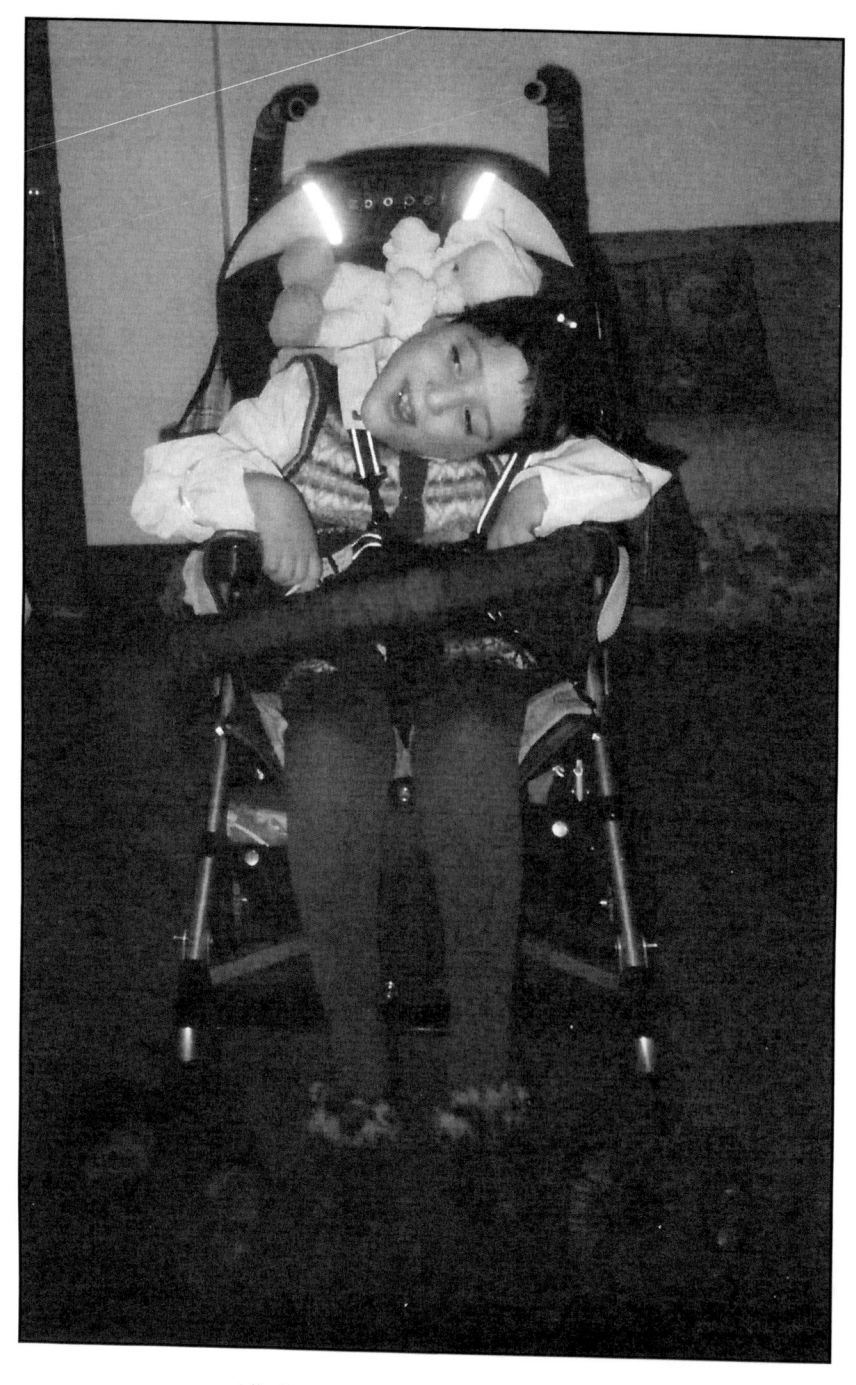

All dressed up for Thanksgiving

My Grandma loves me very much

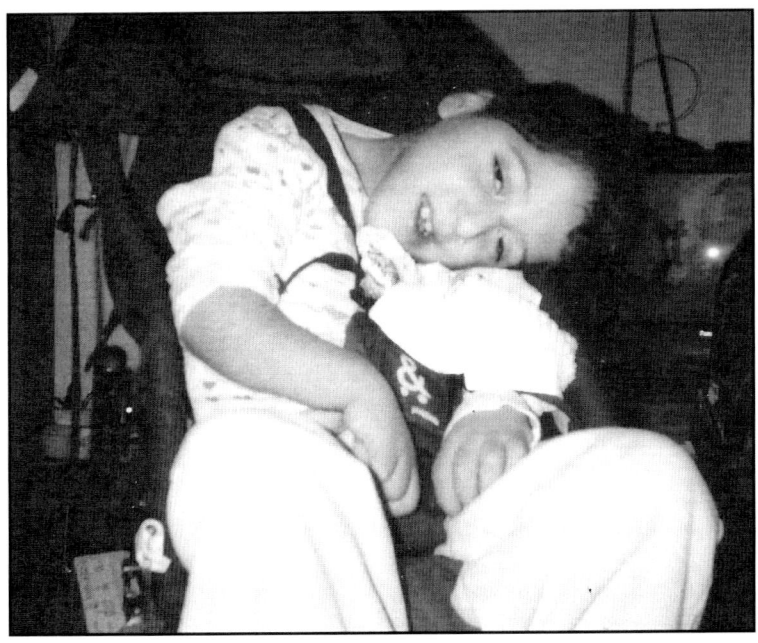

I can't always lift up my head

110 | WHILE HEALING COMES

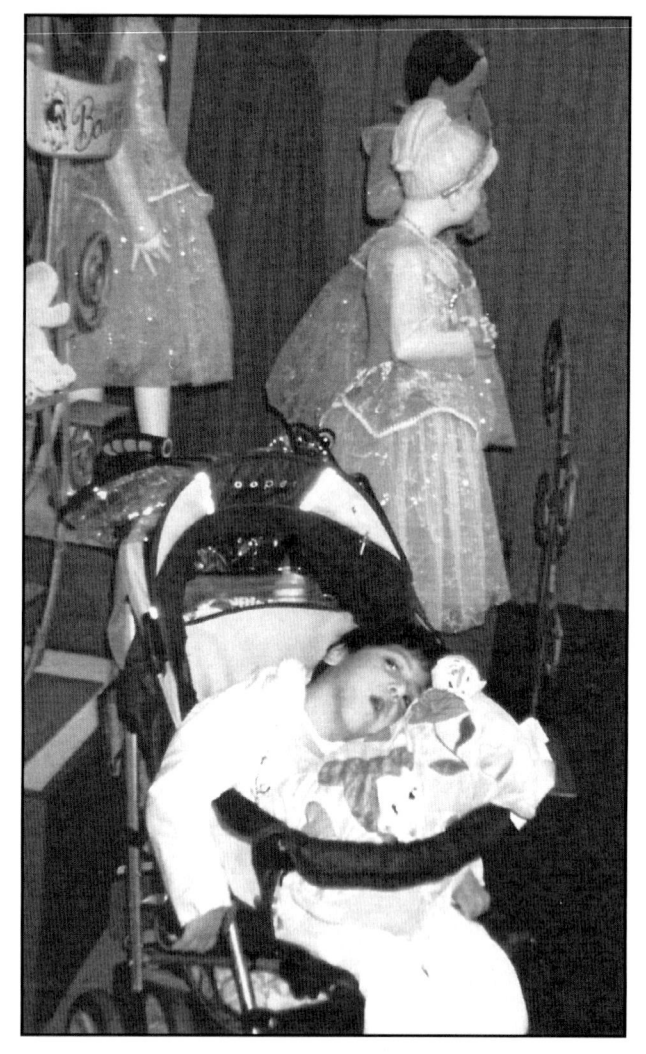

Grandma brought me to see the Disney Princesses

PHOTO GALLERY | 111

Time with my brother, Daniel, always makes me happy

I love my hair this way!

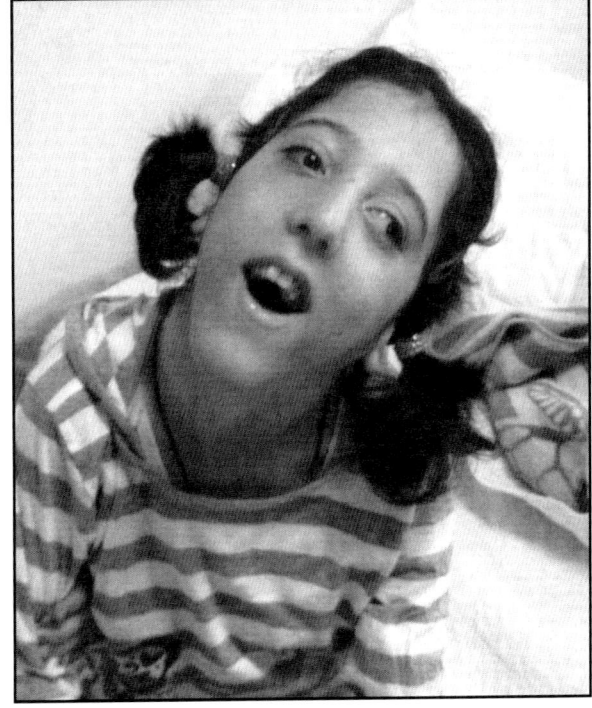

112 | WHILE HEALING COMES

Celebrating my 13th birthday with my brother and cousins

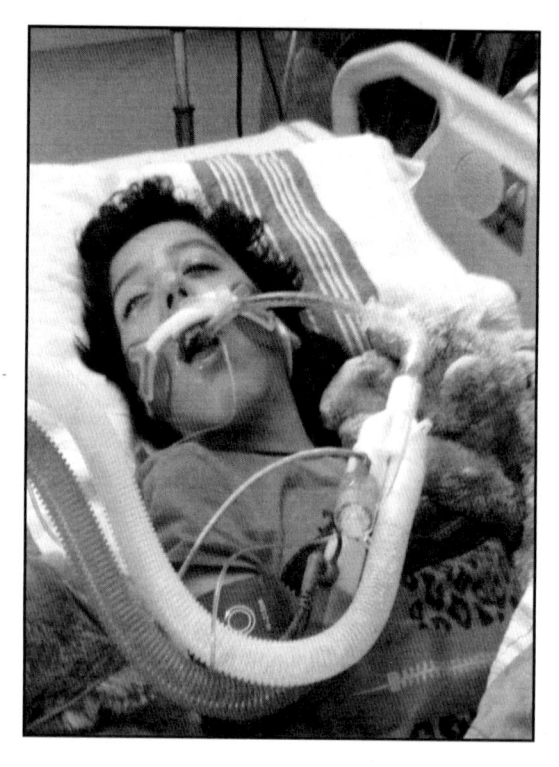

Spending Thanksgiving Day in the hospital

PHOTO GALLERY | 113

Ringing in the New Year!

Prophetic worship with my mom

114 | WHILE HEALING COMES

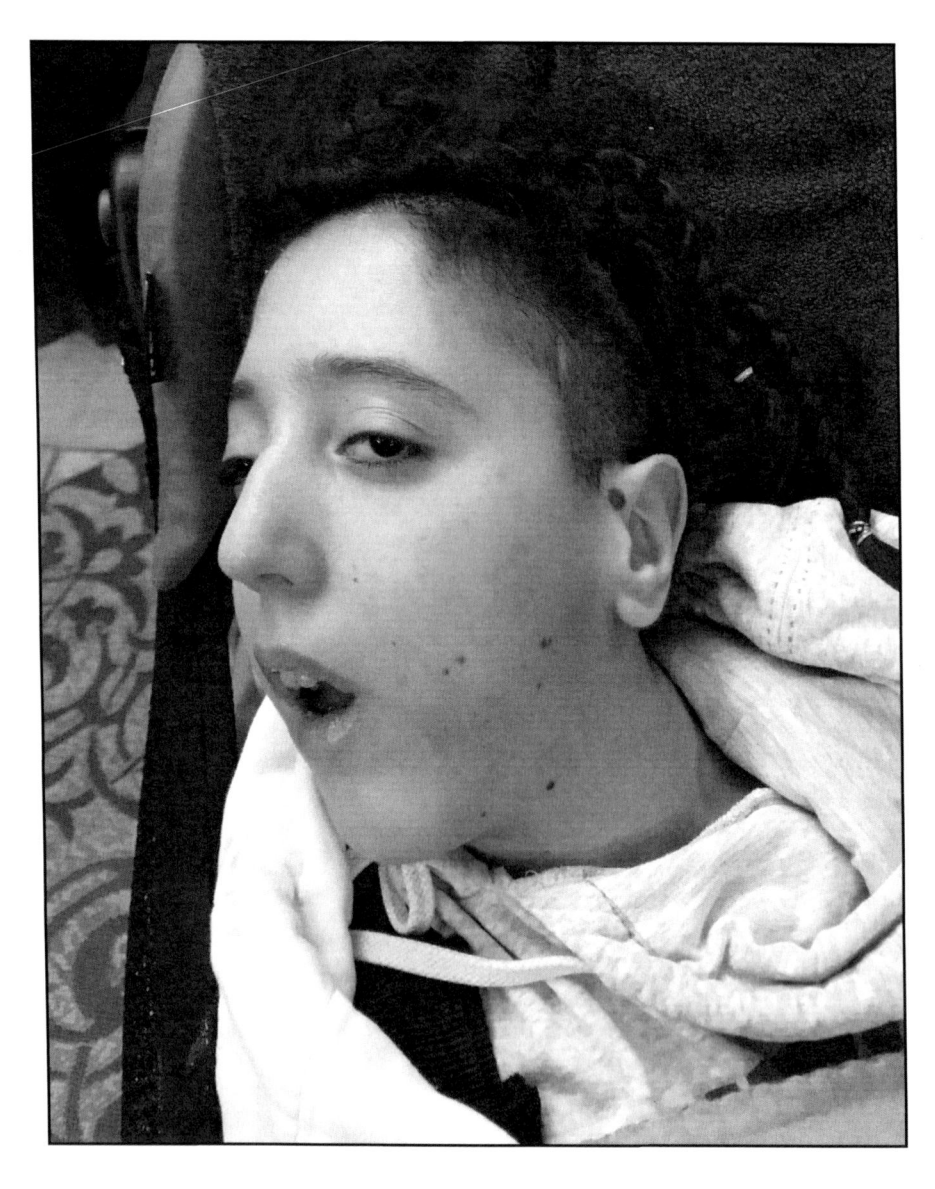

I am so thankful my family loves me and cares for me as I trust God *While Healing Comes* ...

MEET THE AUTHOR

Faye Doudak

> **True freedom cannot be achieved unless a person addresses their obstacles from all three dimensions: physical, emotional, and spiritual.**
>
> —FAYE DOUDAK

You have read our story, so you have learned I am a devoted wife to my husband, Ted, and a mother to four amazing children—one of which has special needs. It has been a challenge to provide all our children with a sense of normalcy, the security of love and affection, and the certainty of being fully present with them all while providing Stephanie with the level of care she requires. Please do not feel sorry for us, we are not victims. Stephanie is a blessing and our family is stronger and better because she is part of it. Our marriage has grown and thrived in the presence of a situation that would break most couples apart. God's grace has surrounded us every single day. His poured out love has filled up our shortcomings, covered our mistakes, and caused our faith to grow deep, unshakable roots.

My heart is to see people live out their potential, allowing nothing to hinder them from realizing all they are meant to be. I try to encourage others to use their gifts to influence their community as they discover and fall in love with who they are.

I am passionate to see people become free from limiting beliefs and enslaving behavior. I am graced to see beyond mistakes, past what is on the surface and recognize a person the way God sees them. I will hold that image of them in my heart and communicate this image to them until they can grab hold of it for themselves and believe what God has revealed about them. My journey with Stephanie has developed this in me and I am grateful. I will do whatever I can to share truth and encourage people to embrace their potential.

As a Doctor of Naturopathy, I am committed to physical, emotional, and spiritual health. My approach to naturopathy has a kingdom influence. In my practice, I help people identify and overcome obstacles that are hindering their health in one or more of these areas. I fully believe in a holistic approach to wellness and know that providing support and accountability through coaching is an effective tool to help others reach their potential.

Through my practice, Wings of Freedom Wellness, I offer support in the following areas:

Physical Support

- Automated Stress Measurements
- Allergy Relief
- Weight Loss Coaching
- Health & Wellness Coaching
- Nutritional Consulting

Emotional Support

- SOZO
- Stress Relief Techniques
- Relief from Emotional Eating
- Life Coaching

Spiritual Support

- SOZO
- Intercessory Prayer
- Prophetic Guidance
- Sharing Jesus with others!

If you would like to connect with me as a naturopath and for a holistic, kingdom approach to addressing and resolving your health issues, please visit:

www.fayedoudak.com

Or check out my facebook page:
Faye Doudak

Faye Doudak
CNHP, ND

Faye Doudak is a Doctor of Naturopathy practicing a holistic, kingdom approach to physical, emotional, and spiritual wellness. She is the mother of four children, one of which has special needs. A woman of great faith, Faye is an inspiring speaker and author, and has her own naturopathy practice, Wings of Freedom Wellness, located in Brooklyn, NY.

Faye offers a number of workshops, a few of which are:

- Breaking Free From Emotional Eating
- Reversing the Symptoms of Autoimmune Diseases
- Providing Support for the Community Surrounding Children With Special Needs

If you would like to book Faye Doudak to speak at your church or organization, please visit:

Faye
DISCOVER YOUR POTENTIAL

www.fayedoudak.com